ACCLAIM FOR *10-MINUTE TALKS*

"Jonathan truly understands youth and how to minister to them. He also knows how to communicate Scripture to youth in high-impact ways. *10-Minute Talks* is filled with messages that do exactly that."

—Dan Kimball, author, *They Like Jesus but Not the Church: Insights from Emerging Generations*

"Don't make the mistake of thinking this is another book of quickie ideas for microwave youth work: 10 minutes of prep time and 10 minutes of mush that has about 10 minutes of impact in a student's life! I know a lot of youth workers will find this book really helpful. Good stuff!"

—Duffy Robbins, author, *Speaking to Teenagers*; professor of youth ministry, Eastern University

"Good, tight talks to teenagers are a challenge, if not an art form. Jonathan's book not only supplies practical outlines and stories that make this task much easier, it teaches a way of thinking about talks that you'll carry with you into a fruitful ministry anywhere."

—Dr. Dave Rahn, senior vice president and chief ministry officer, Youth for Christ/USA

"It seems as though books about how to do 'talks' are a dime a dozen. Not this one. *10-Minute Talks* is full of material that flat out works. If you're a youth worker who'd rather spend time ministering to students than Googling the latest lesson outlines and illustrations, *10-Minutes Talks* is exactly what you need."

—Greg Stier, president, Dare 2 Share Ministries

"Few things have greater power than a story. Jonathan McKee has gathered some unforgettable stories that can provide a foundation for presenting life-changing truth. If you only have 10 minutes, this may be what you need to make every one of them count."

—Ken Davis, author, *How to Speak to Youth ... and Keep Them Awake at the Same Time*

MORE

10-MINUTE TALKS

JONATHAN MCKEE
with Thomas W. McKee

MORE

10-MINUTE TALKS

24 Messages Your Students Will Love

 ZONDERVAN®

ZONDERVAN.com/
AUTHORTRACKER
follow your favorite authors

 youth specialties

ZONDERVAN

More 10-Minute Talks
Copyright © 2012 by Jonathan McKee

YS Youth Specialties is a trademark of YOUTHWORKS!, INCORPORATED and is registered with the United States Patent and Trademark Office.

This title is also available as a Zondervan ebook. Visit www.zondervan.com/ebooks.

Requests for information should be addressed to:

Zondervan, *Grand Rapids, Michigan 49530*

Library of Congress Cataloging-in-Publication Data

McKee, Jonathan R. (Jonathan Ray), 1970-
        More 10-minute talks : 24 messages your students will love / Jonathan McKee ; with Thomas W. McKee.
            pages cm
        ISBN 978-0-310-69290-4 (softcover)
        1. Church work with youth. 2. Youth—Religious life. I. McKee, Thomas W. II. Title.
    BV4447.M238 2013
    268'.433—dc23   2012036110

Cover design: SharpSeven Design
Interior design: Mark Novelli and Matthew Van Zomeren

Printed in the United States of America

12 13 14 15 16 17 18 /DCI/ 22 21 20 19 18 17 16 15 14 13 12 11 10 9 8 7 6 5 4 3 2 1

ACKNOWLEDGMENTS

"For what we preach is not ourselves, but Jesus Christ as Lord." (2 Corinthians 4:5)

Jesus deserves all the credit and glory for anything good that happens as a result of this book. If anything bad happens...that was probably me.

Like the first *10-Minute Talks* book, my dad deserves more than just an acknowledgment in this one—which is why this time his name is on the cover with my name. If you've ever heard my dad speak, then you know what a huge addition he is to this book. He helped me with so much of the research that went into these stories and was a great help with many of the wrap-ups. He truly cowrote this with me. Thanks Dad.

Authors always thank their spouses and kids, but until you've written a book and seen the "trickle down" that flows to the family (e.g., the trickle down of time spent writing and not hanging with the family, the trickle down with stress during deadlines), you know that the family often pays the price with the author. So with incredible thanks and sincerity, much love to my wife Lori and my three kids: Alec, Alyssa, and Ashley. I love you all so much!

Thank you to all those who partner with our ministry, The Source for Youth Ministry. David R. Smith, Todd Pearage...you guys are always an encouragement and offer great input for my books. U rock!

And a big shout-out to all my friends who provided me with ideas, feedback, and final tweaks. Thanks Mark Oestreicher, Greg Alderman, and even my son Alec with his youthful insights and mad editing skills!

CONTENTS

Why 10 Minutes?   11

10-Minute Tips: How to Use This Book   17

Section One: Spiritual Growth Talks (listed by title/topic)

Talk #1: But It's Only a Knee/Spiritual Gifts, Unity   23

Talk #2: Three Seconds/Forgiveness, Mercy   31

Talk #3: Keeping the Goal in Sight...Even When
You Can't See It/Focus on Christ, Faith   43

Talk #4: From Goals to Wells/Vision, Gifts, Giving   52

Talk #5: Five Choices Ago/Temptation, Sin   60

Talk #6: I Don't Belong/Reaching Out to Others, Evangelism   71

Talk #7: Jethro/Dealing with Hardships   80

Talk #8: Ignoring the Signs/Warnings, Pride, Temptation   91

Talk #9: A Lifetime of Decisions/Decision-Making   99

Talk #10: Surrender/Surrendering to God   107

Talk #11: A Second Chance/Social Justice, Missions, Fresh Start   117

Talk #12: Socks/Faith, Trust, Suffering   127

Section Two: Outreach Talks (listed by title/topic)

Talk #13: The Traps of Success/Success, Seeking Satisfaction   141

Talk #14: The Miracle of Forgiveness/Forgiveness   151

Talk #15: It's Not Hurting Anybody/Warnings,
Consequences, Excuses   159

Talk #16: Ruined, Rescued, and Restored/Redemption,
Restoration   167

Talk #17: Wall Guy/Our Foundation, Resurrection of Christ   175

Talk #18: Nobody's Perfect/Mercy, Grace, Forgiveness   186

Talk #19: Somebody Up There Is Looking Out for Me/God
Reveals Himself to Us   196

Talk #20: Escaping Death/Death, Eternal Life   205

Talk #21: Jackson's Hole/Stuff, Temporary Versus Eternal   216

Talk #22: Unbroken/New Life, Forgiveness, Freedom
from Bitterness   230

Talk #23: Let Go/True Faith, Surrendering to God   240

Talk #24: Sparing Francis/Salvation, Sacrifice   251

WHY **10** MINUTES?
A DESPERATE NEED FOR CLEAR, CONCISE COMMUNICATION

It's evident to everyone in the room...except the speaker.

The audience is bored, retaining very little, and can't wait for the speaker to just stop talking.

Sure, they'll remember a funny story, maybe even the Scripture the speaker used...but the main point of the talk? No one's sure. Did it have something to do with the story of the cat and the aluminum foil?

Talented speaker Ken Davis conducted a survey for his book, *Secrets of Dynamic Communication*, of 2,500 people leaving church services when the sermon should have remained fresh in their minds. Well, 70 percent had "no idea what had just been communicated." Of the remaining 30 percent, some could remember a joke or a story, but few could identify any purpose or direction of the sermons.

The study gets worse. Ken also interviewed the speakers themselves. More than half "could not articulate in a simple sentence any objective or focus to their talk."

No wonder no one remembered the main point.

What's the common denominator here?

Communicating with Clarity

I do a lot of speaking. From California to D.C., Texas to Nova Scotia. School assemblies, camps, conferences. Wiry middle-school tweens, over-philosophical college students, blue-haired little old ladies.

I also do a lot of listening. I attend lots of conferences, I'm in church on Sundays, and I usually hear a regular dose of midweek talks in youth ministries I visit across the United States. And in the last decade I've listened to literally hundreds of speakers apply to be part of a speakers' network we offered through our ministry.

We added fewer than 30.

As a result of all my listening over the years, I've made an observation about the majority of youth workers' speaking abilities: Most could use some help communicating with clarity.

Let me ask two simple questions:

ONE: On average, how long do you talk when giving a sermon/message?

TWO: Why?

No matter what your answer is to the first question, chances are good you've never thought about an answer to the second question. In fact, most speakers have never thought to ask themselves that question. So let me ask you another question:

Why do we talk for 45 minutes when we can say it in 10?

Length

The following are two scenarios in which important messages were communicated clearly. The first comes from our youth room; the second comes from a field in Pennsylvania.

Last month, Jaime, a 22-year-old college student, walked to the front of our youth ministry room and opened with these words:

Last year I realized that the friends I've surrounded myself with were dragging me down, so I made one of the toughest decisions I've ever made...

For the next five minutes she shared a single story of how surrounding herself with the wrong crowd led to disaster. Then she shared a Scripture out of Hebrews 12 that encourages believers to surround themselves with people of encouragement—people who'll help us with our faith walk, not hinder it. Then she closed with these words: *Think of the handful of people you spend the most time with: Are they drawing you closer to Christ...or dragging you away from him?*

Then she sat down. She spoke for five minutes and 22 seconds. That's all.

Let me ask you another question: Would her talk have been any better had she blabbed on for another 40 minutes?

As you ponder your answer, here's the other story...the one from a field in Pennsylvania.

It was November 19, 1863. Four months earlier, the Battle of Gettysburg claimed almost 8,000 American lives. It was the turning point in the Civil War—such an important victory for the Union that President Abraham Lincoln decided to address the country from the blood-soaked field.

It was a circus. Almost 20,000 gathered for the event. Edward Everett, a former senator and president of Harvard, spoke for more than two hours.

Then Abraham Lincoln, a bit under the weather, slowly walked to the podium:

Four score and seven years ago our fathers brought forth...

Two minutes later, he was done.

Two minutes!

Now another question: Have you ever heard or read what Everett talked about? Did you even know he "opened" for Abe?

Likely, no.

Like every other American from that historical day to the present, you were more impacted by the (much) shorter speech.

The best speakers know that impact isn't determined by length of speech.

Want more proof? Martin Luther King, Jr.'s famous "I Have a Dream" speech lasted just 16 minutes. Franklin D. Roosevelt kept his "Day of Infamy" speech to just six and a half minutes. Winston Churchill's "Never Give In" speech was just over four minutes long.

Okay, let's go back to the second question: "Why?"

Jaime, Lincoln, and Dr. King were aware of their audiences and the occasions. Edward Everett probably didn't care. He wanted to be heard... and consequently wasn't.

So think through your audience and the occasion.

And let's learn an important lesson: Clarity and impact don't require length.

Oh, I can hear it now...

Jonathan, I can't believe you're encouraging youth pastors to water down the message of the gospel!

We shouldn't cater to our culture's short attention span.

But Andy Stanley and Francis Chan talk for 45 minutes. Why can't I?

There are some wacky assumptions in those statements. For starters, short does NOT equal watered down. More importantly, Stanley and Chan are one in a million (well, two). They are amazing communicators. They can easily get away with 45 minutes...and if we're being honest, most of us can't.

You've sat through youth talks that lasted longer than the most recent Lord of the Rings film...director's edition. Painful. Some youth workers and speakers tend to equate LONG with DEEP.

Not the case.

In most situations, LONG equates with BORING.

One Story, One Passage...One Clear Point

Don't get me wrong. Gifted speakers can (and should) teach 30-minute expository messages, even to teens. The problem? Many who give those 30-minute talks (and unfortunately the 45-minute talks) are like *American Idol* contestants who hear "no" from three judges while arguing, "But all my friends say I'm an amazing singer!"

So if you aren't Stanley or Chan...take heart. You're in good company. Most of us aren't.

But you can still communicate with clarity, especially when you focus on one story, one passage, and one clear point.

That's probably part of the reason I've been teaching a workshop titled, "Speaking to Teenagers with Short Attention Spans" at the National Youth Workers Convention for the last few years. A bunch of us are responsible to speak on regular occasions in our ministries...and clear, story-based 10-minute talks are often just what the doctor ordered.

So don't feel as though you have to speak for 45 minutes just because the guy preaching in your favorite weekly podcast does so. Again, long talks aren't always deeper talks. Long talks aren't more effective just because they're long. Therefore a 10-minute talk might be just the tool you need to communicate the truth with clarity.

That's exactly what we've provided for you in this book—24 story-based talks that communicate one passage and one point clearly.

10-MINUTE TIPS
HOW TO USE THIS BOOK

How exactly do you make a point in 10 minutes?

Good stories.

They're powerful teaching tools. I'm sure you don't need convincing to use the same method Jesus used in his teaching. Good, relevant stories paint pictures and hold the attention of the toughest crowds. Some of the best talks I've heard have been based on a single story with one point—resulting in one powerful impact.

That's the goal of this book.

Each of these 10-minute talks includes one story teaching one clear point, using one passage of Scripture. Some may be a little shorter than 10 minutes and some a minute or two longer. You can adapt them as necessary. And who knows? They might even spark the memory of stories from your own life you can use instead—which is even better!

The talks are divided into two categories:

1. **Spiritual Growth Talks**—for teenagers who already have relationships with Christ but need to grow in their faith.
2. **Outreach Talks**—for teenagers who don't know Christ and need to hear the gospel message.

Each talk provides you with several elements:

Title

Topic(s)

Big Idea: The one point the talk communicates, usually in the form of a sound bite.

Scripture: The chosen Bible passage.

Particulars: Specifics about the story, such as background and even hints on how to tell it (if the talk is unusually short or long, you'll see a note indicating as much).

Story: The bulk of the talk.

Transition Statement: Helps you segue from the story to the Big Idea (you'll want to rehearse this—good transition statements carry your audience smoothly to the Big Idea).

Application and Scripture: Verbalizing the Big Idea and sharing the scriptural foundation.

Closing: Closing statement, application, and prayer or call to respond.

Small Group Questions: The addition of small groups helps young people process what they've heard and dialogue about it. Each set of questions starts with a simple question that you ask **Around the Circle** of your group (i.e., it requires feedback from everyone in the group). The rest of the questions are labeled **Ask Just a Few** (questions that don't require everyone to answer) or **Around the Circle**. (It's key to use **Around the Circle** questions to help shy kids open up...and loud kids to shut up!)

Don't let all the categories scare you. Just follow the four tips in the next section, and you'll gain skills to tell memorable stories and bring home biblical truth loud and clear.

FOUR SIMPLE TIPS TO HELP YOU EFFECTIVELY USE THESE TALKS

1. Memorize the Talk

Don't worry—you don't have to memorize it word for word. Think of the talk as a joke you just heard. How many times have you heard a joke, and the next day you turned around and told it to someone else? Memorize these talks just like that.

In many situations you won't need every detail—just the main storyline. For example, in the talk, "Five Choices Ago," you could probably read or hear it once and then turn around and tell the story flawlessly yourself. The details aren't that important—you can even change them up a bit. Just rehearse the transition, the Scripture, and the application.

But other talks (e.g., "But It's Only a Knee," the story of Derrick Rose, with all his basketball stats) might take more effort to memorize. We don't want to invent history! When it comes to the part with Rose's statistics, don't feel bad pulling out a notecard with his accomplishments listed in bullets.

But be warned: Don't let this become a slippery slope leading you to use notes as a crutch for the entire story. The point of memorization is to free yourself from the handcuffs of notes, which can allow your story to flow naturally.

2. Practice the talk out loud at least once.

I'm recommending this as a bare minimum. I rehearse these stories numerous times to perfect my transitions and get a feel for my own timing. One person did a trial run of one of these talks, and it took him just eight minutes. Another guy giving the same talk took 20 minutes (he really stretched it out).

Many of these talks have that flexibility. You might conclude that some stories carry too many details, so be flexible there. If you like details, use them. But feel free to omit statistics, scores, years, and average wind speed if those details seem superfluous.

Bottom line: Evaluate your needs, consider your time limitations, and adjust accordingly. Just keep in mind that practicing these talks out loud gives you these options.

3. Master your landmarks.

I always say this to speakers I train: "Make sure you have a captivating beginning, polished transitions, and a powerful ending." If you're in a rush and decide to skip practicing a talk out loud, then at least practice your first three lines, your transition statement, and your closing. The other details can settle into this framework.

4. Bathe it in prayer.

Don't go it alone. God doesn't need our help to change lives, but God has allowed us to be part of the process. And one of our jobs is to keep praying (in addition to talking).

SECTION ONE:
SPIRITUAL GROWTH TALKS

TALK 01

TITLE: BUT IT'S ONLY A KNEE

TOPICS: Spiritual Gifts, Unity

BIG IDEA: Just as one knee dashed the Chicago Bulls' hopes for a basketball championship, an injury to one part of God's body, the church, leads to suffering for the whole church.

SCRIPTURE

> If one part suffers, every part suffers with it;
> if one part is honored, every part rejoices with it.
> (1 Corinthians 12:26)

PARTICULARS

Rose's injury powerfully illustrates Paul's teaching on spiritual gifts and the importance of each part of the body. The story starts with game one of the first round of the 2012 NBA playoffs when Chicago's best player, Derrick Rose, suffered a season-ending knee injury. There's a lot of information about Rose, his accomplishments, etc., but the most important element is his "mental" attitude—especially when you draw the analogy between the mind and the knee in the application section.

Derrick isn't perfect. Like most NBA players (and all of us), he's made mistakes. You may choose to mention that when you talk about him. This talk was written in 2012, so by the time you share this story, who knows where Rose will be? (Make sure you update his whereabouts and recovery progress.)

STORY

It was 2012 and Chicago basketball fans tasted victory. This could very well be the Bulls' year.

The city hadn't been so excited about the team since the glory days of Michael Jordan. Now they were back to the top position in the NBA's Eastern Conference and poised to go all the way.

In game one of the first round of the playoffs, the Bulls led the 76ers by 12 points. With only a minute left in the game, a player went down, and the raucous crowd was instantly silenced as Derrick Rose was helped off the court.

Basketball fans around the world waited to hear the fate of Derrick... and the fate of the Bulls, as many said Derrick had led the team to the 2012 playoffs.

You might say Derrick Rose was meant to play basketball. He was born in Chicago in 1988 and raised on the south side where his three talented older brothers played the game. They were raised watching and idolizing Michael Jordan, and they tutored Derrick on local courts. As Derrick grew up, he drew more attention in the Chicago area. His mother saw his potential as an NBA player, so she was very strict with him, making sure he kept away from wild parties and gangs.

Derrick had a stellar high school basketball career at Simeon Career Academy. In his junior year he led the Wolverines to a state title. The team was nationally ranked, and Rose was awarded all-state honors. Rose was noticed by universities around the country.

As Rose began his senior year, he was ranked the fifth-best prospect in the nation by *Sports Illustrated*. With Rose leading the way, Simeon became the first Chicago public league school to win two straight state championships. The team was ranked number one in the nation by *Sports Illustrated* as Rose averaged 25.2 points per game.

When Rose was part of a team, it won championships. He was on his way.

Rose accepted a scholarship to play for the University of Memphis Tigers because of its reputation for getting their players to the NBA. With Rose on the team, the Tigers claimed a number-one ranking for the first time in 25 years. Memphis was the number-one seed in the college playoffs, dominating teams on their way to the Final Four. But they lost to the University of Kansas Jayhawks in overtime in the NCAA championship game.

A month later Rose declared for the 2008 draft. He was selected first overall by the Chicago Bulls. He took Rookie of the Year honors, and then made the all-star team his second year. Each year since Rose became a pro, he's led the Bulls to the NBA playoffs. In 2011 he was the youngest player ever to win the NBA's Most Valuable Player award, joining Michael Jordan as the only Chicago Bulls players to win the honor.

Even though Rose was an all star his second season (2010), he knew he had to improve his game. He worked with his personal trainer to improve his jump shot, his three-point game, his free throws, and reading defenses better. Rose was known for his work ethic, but he took it to a whole new level that summer. Rose's mentality was, "I'm pretty good, but I need to be better."

And that summer paid off. After hitting 16 three-pointers in each of his first two NBA seasons, Rose made 128 three-pointers in his third season. But best of all Rose's confidence was up. When he missed his three-point shots in previous years, he would back off on his shooting. But in his third year Rose just kept shooting, and he led the Bulls to the top seed in the Eastern Conference.

Rose was the Bulls' new shining star.

Derrick's teammates loved him. They said he was humble, and they followed someone like that—great player, strong work ethic, humble attitude, vocal leader. What a combination.

But all of his dreams—and all of Chicago's dreams—came crashing down with Rose lying on the floor of the United Center.

The audience watched as Rose reached down and grabbed his knee.

As he was helped off the court, people felt the loss of their star and their hopes of a championship were in question...all because of a knee!

The MRI revealed that Rose tore the ACL in his left knee and would miss the rest of the season. Without Rose, Chicago only won one more game of the first playoff round, and the number-one team did not advance. Miami ended up winning everything that year...a year that might have been Chicago's.

All because of a knee.

TRANSITION STATEMENT

One knee put Rose out of the lineup for perhaps an entire year. The loss of this one player seemingly ended Chicago's run for a championship.

One player.

One knee.

APPLICATION AND SCRIPTURE

When I think of Derrick's knee injury, I'm reminded of the words of the Apostle Paul, who often uses sports analogies in his letters (the good fight, running the race, etc.). Paul writes about the parts of the body and how important each part is. He uses the illustration of the hand and foot. If Paul had watched Chicago during the first game of the NBA playoffs, he might have used the knee as an illustration. Listen to what Paul says about the parts of the body.

If one part suffers, every part suffers with it; if one part is honored, every part rejoices with it. (1 Corinthians 12:26)

In 1 Corinthians 12, Paul uses a bit of humor to get his point across. He creates this scenario where the body parts are talking to each other. It's almost like an animated film where the ear is talking to the hand or foot. So let's imagine I am Paul sitting in Chicago's game one of the NBA playoffs. In my hotel room that night (although Paul would have probably been sitting in jail, as that's where he wrote a lot of his letters) I write to the church in Chicago (Corinth) and say something like this:

Can the mind say to the knee, "You are not important. You are only a knee. But I am the great mind that reads defenses. I can change the whole game by my attitude. I can think. You are just a knee; you can't think. But I can miss the first seven shots of a game, and as the mind, I can decide that I will keep shooting. But you can't make a decision. You can't set up the pick-and-roll. You are just a knee"?

Paul pushes the comical analogy and draws the conclusion, "If the body was all 'mind,' how can the arms and hands make the shot? The mind needs the arms, hands, legs and the knees." Listen to what Paul says:

[14]Even so the body is not made up of one part but of many.

[15]Now if the foot should say, "Because I am not a hand, I do not belong to the body," it would not for that reason stop being part of the body. [16]And if the ear should say, "Because I am not an eye, I do not belong to the body," it would not for that reason stop being part of the body. [17]If the whole body were an eye, where would the sense of hearing be? If the whole body were an ear, where would the sense of smell be? [18]But in fact God has placed the parts in the body, every one of them, just as he wanted them to be. [19]If they were all one part, where would the body be? [20]As it is, there are many parts, but one body.

[21]The eye cannot say to the hand, "I don't need you!" And the head cannot say to the feet, "I don't need you!" (1 Corinthians 12:14-21)

Paul uses this analogy to demonstrate that we are all important. Derrick Rose improved his game. He worked on his shooting, his mental game and his leadership, but without a knee, all of that would come to an end not only for himself, but all of Chicago. To be a complete player, Derrick needed the mind and the knees. He needed the whole body. When one part suffered, the whole body (and team) suffered.

Think about our youth group. We have many parts. Too often we feel, "Oh, I just run the soundboard. I'm not a leader, or guitar player, or singer, or speaker. Those are the up-front people everyone knows and admires. But I'm just a quiet kid who loves to serve."

Too often we don't notice the person who operates the soundboard until the electricity goes out, or the person misses a cue and the mic doesn't work. Then we all notice. The sound guy is important.

Too often we don't notice the quiet girl in the back who is a servant of God, who lives her faith authentically and has reached many of her friends. You'll probably never see her on stage, but she is just as important.

Paul uses the analogy of the body and the many parts of the body to demonstrate that every part is important. We can't say that the eye, or the hand, or the ear, or the foot is most important. They each have their role. Just ask Derrick Rose and he will tell you how important the knee is to all of his game. Without the knee, he didn't play.

And without you, the whole body suffers.

God has given to each of us talents and special gifts, which play important roles in our church and youth group. It is wrong for us to think that we are too important, or not important to the body. Every part is significant, and when one part is missing, we all hurt.

CLOSING

So what? What does this mean?

First, know your part in the body of Christ. Read 1 Corinthians 12-14 and discover the gifts that God has given us. What would God have you do and be in our group? We want to help you discover your gifts and roles. If you are wondering what your role is, please talk to us. One of my roles is to help you discover your gifts of the body.

Second, take an active part in your role. When you don't, we all are hurting.

And third, it is important that we keep affirming everyone's role, not just the upfront leaders. We need to affirm them also, but let's not forget the other important parts that make us whole.

Let's pray.

SMALL GROUP QUESTIONS

1. **Around the Circle:** What is your favorite sport to watch or play?

2. **Ask Just a Few:** How important was Derrick Rose's knee to Chicago?

3. **Ask Just a Few:** What happens when one part of "the body of Christ" suffers?

In 1 Corinthians 12:21, Paul says:

The eye cannot say to the hand, "I don't need you!" And the head cannot say to the feet, "I don't need you!"

4. **Ask Just a Few:** What is Paul trying to get across in this passage?

5. **Ask Just a Few:** What are some of the important "parts" of our group? Do any of these get ignored or deemed less important?

6. **Around the Circle:** What are some of the gifts that God has given you?

7. **Around the Circle:** How can God use your gifts for his purpose?

8. **Around the Circle:** What is one thing you can do this week to use your gifts for God? How can I, as your youth group leader, help you do that?

TALK 02

TITLE: THREE SECONDS

TOPICS: Forgiveness, Mercy

BIG IDEA: There is a new math of grace and mercy that begins when we give to others the forgiveness that God has given to us. We need to forgive others, just as God forgave us.

SCRIPTURE

> [32]"Then the master called the servant in. 'You wicked servant,' he said, 'I canceled all that debt of yours because you begged me to. [33]Shouldn't you have had mercy on your fellow servant just as I had on you?' [34]In anger his master handed him over to the jailers to be tortured, until he should pay back all he owed.
>
> [35]"This is how my heavenly Father will treat each of you unless you forgive your brother or sister from your heart." (Matthew 18:32-35)

PARTICULARS

This story is a modern teenage version of the parable of the unmerciful servant. Most young people won't recognize the story until you make the connection.

STORY

Julia had an easy senior year. She had paid her dues her whole life, getting good grades throughout, and getting most of her tough courses over within the first three years of high school. Now she only had four classes and an early dismissal each day.

Her four classes were a joke this semester. She had English, Weight Training, Government, and finally, during fourth period she was a Teacher's Assistant, or TA, for her favorite teacher, Mrs. Smith.

Julia met Mrs. Smith her freshman year when she played volleyball. Coach Smith was an amazing volleyball coach and had brought Julia's team to sectionals several years in a row. Julia had been on weekend trips with the volleyball team each year and really got to know her coach. Every player loved Coach and respected her.

Volleyball season was over this semester, but Julia managed to get weight training and the TA position with Coach Smith. Julia loved this because Coach always took care of her volleyball players.

Julia had learned more from Coach Smith than any adult in her life. What Julia didn't realize was that the biggest lesson she would ever learn was just around the corner.

This particular Monday didn't seem different than any other Monday, but Julia made a series of poor decisions early in the day that set the course for events she would remember the rest of her life.

It started when Julia and her friend Maddy finished their English test with half of first period remaining. Julia and Maddy were both A students and had just aced another test. Mrs. Ryan didn't have anything else for them that period so she asked the two girls if they would do her a favor and return some media equipment to Mrs. Havard in the journalism room. Mrs. Ryan gave them a free pass of sorts, saying, "And when you finish, if you'd like to just hang out in the journalism room on the computers for the rest of the period, that's fine."

Julia and Maddy returned the equipment in a matter of minutes and found themselves relaxing on the journalism couches with three of the yearbook students. Mrs. Havard rarely even came into the classroom, so all the students were unsupervised.

Julia was excited because Josh Davis was hanging on the couch with her...and Josh was gorgeous! Unfortunately, Britney Kensington was one of the other students on the couch. Julia knew her from fourth period where she was a TA. Britney was a junior who always disrespected Julia and often prompted other girls to do the same. Julia loathed Britney.

But that didn't matter very much at the moment, because Josh wasn't talking with Britney. He was talking with Julia and Maddy.

Julia had always liked Josh, but most girls did. Josh was one of the star baseball players at their school and was often homecoming king or some kind of royalty at the dances. Both Julia and Maddy had numerous classes with Josh over the years. He was always fun to hang out with. Right now he was talking about some recently released song he just downloaded. Julia didn't really care; she was just enjoying the fact that he was talking with them.

Josh stopped and searched through his backpack. "Where's my phone?" He started pulling books out, searching the bottom of his backpack. Then he stopped short and looked up as if recalling something. "Ah! I left it in my car."

He leaned in closer to Maddy and Julia. "Come out to my car real quick while I get my phone."

This wasn't a big deal. Even though students weren't allowed in the parking lot during school, they did it all the time. Before Julia even had a chance to respond, Maddy said, "Sure," leaping from the couch and grabbing Julia's hand. Before Julia knew it, the three of them were in the parking lot by Josh's little white Sentra.

"Get in real quick before someone sees us; I wanna play you that song I downloaded this morning."

Maddy hopped in the front seat, and without thinking much about it, Julia hopped in the back seat.

Josh found his iPhone in the center console and plugged it in to his Sentra's iPod jack and cranked up the volume. It was a new song from Wiz Khalifa. Josh pulled something out of his jacket and put it in his mouth. Then he pulled out a lighter and lit it up. After a long drag, Josh exhaled smoke into the small cabin of the car. The windows were closed so no one could hear them.

Julia couldn't believe that Josh was smoking pot. She would have never guessed.

"What are you doing?" Julia finally asked.

Maddy laughed. "Whadaya think he's doing?" And she grabbed the joint and took a long hit.

"Maddy!" Julia pled.

Maddy reached back, offering a hit to Julia. Julia had never been offered drugs before. She had seen the commercials, and she had heard the lectures in health class. This was it. This was that moment she had heard about since she was in fifth grade.

"No thanks," Julia said politely. Then she pointed to the gum in her mouth. "Gum."

There was an awkward pause for a few seconds, then all three of them burst out laughing.

"Gum," Josh repeated.

Every minute that passed, Josh seemed to find things funnier. It was pretty amusing for Julia to watch. That's probably why she lost track of time. She looked down at her phone.

9:10.

Second period started at 8:55.

"Oh crap!" Julia blurted, opening the door and hopping out of the smoke-filled Sentra. "We're late for weight training."

Josh burst out laughing. But Maddy didn't.

"Crap. Crap. Craaaaaaaaap!" Maddy groaned. She hopped out of the front seat. Both girls said goodbye to Josh, who just sat there laughing in the front seat. Then they sprinted toward the gym.

"Got any more gum?" Maddy asked as they ran down the last hall-way almost reaching the gym.

Julia grabbed a piece from her purse and tossed it to Maddy in one quick motion. Then the girls ran into the gym where the rest of the girls were already lined up and dressed down for weight training.

Suddenly 63 heads turned and looked at the girls, but Julia only noticed one. Coach Smith had looked up from her clipboard and had a really confused look on her face. She blew a whistle and told the class to begin their stretches, then she walked over to the two late arrivals.

When Coach got about five feet from them she stopped, tilted her head, and changed her expression. "Weed?" she asked in disbelief. Coach Smith had grown up with a brother who smoked pot incessantly. She knew the smell well.

"In my office," Coach said firmly.

The two girls followed Coach into her office, exchanging a quick scared look at each other before passing through the threshold.

"Julia and Maddy," Coach said with disappointment in her voice. "I don't even know what to say." Coach plopped in her chair and began massaging her temples as if a migraine was coming on.

Julia literally dropped to her knees and started crying. "I'm so sorry, Coach. I swear. I didn't smoke anything. I was just in the parking lot..."

Coach interrupted her. "The parking lot? You know the rules."

"I know. I know," Julia continued. "A guy invited me and Maddy there. He was all, 'Come listen to this song I downloaded,' and Mrs. Ryan had let us out. Honestly. I didn't even think about it. I just wanted to hear the song and next thing I knew he was smoking..."

Coach turned her head away like she didn't want to hear anymore, and she held out her hand in a motion that said, "Stop talking."

Silence hung in the room like a dense fog. The ticking of the clock on the wall seemed to increase in volume. Seconds felt like hours.

The girls didn't dare say a word. They felt like the next person that spoke would be sure to perish.

Finally Coach broke the silence: "Don't ever do this again!"

The girls exhaled like they had been holding their breath for hours.

"Wait," Coach continued, holding up her hand again, "I'm not finished. You guys broke the rules. You were tardy, you were in the parking lot, you came into my class smelling like weed with a story that I can only hope is true...I'm probably an idiot for not sending you both to Mr. Ramos right now."

She paused again, contemplating her next words. "But I know both of you. I know you're good girls. I know this was probably just a stupid mistake. And I know I wouldn't want one stupid mistake costing my future."

Her next words surprised Julia.

"So I forgive you."

Coach's volume increased and she slowed down her speech, emphasizing every word. "Just remember that you received mercy today. Don't ever pull this again!"

The girls both hugged Coach and then rushed to their lockers to change.

Julia had been given the best gift in the world: mercy.

A couple hours later Julia was back in the gym, this time holding the attendance clipboard. This was the normal routine for Julia's fourth period as the TA for Coach Smith. Coach was in her office ordering some equipment, so Julia was handling roll call by herself today.

Most of the girls had already gathered for class when the second bell rang. The rule was that students had to be inside the gym by the second bell. Mrs. Smith always started the year pretty strict, but then she lightened up as the semester went on, especially if a student came in the door just a few seconds late.

Julia looked up at the door when the bell finished ringing, and three seconds later Britney Kensington ran in.

Julia cringed at the sight of her. This girl had made her life miserable.

"You're late," Julia pronounced.

Britney's jaw dropped like she had just been accused of grand larceny. "What? Like three seconds?"

Julia felt powerful. "The rule is that you have to be in the gym when the second bell rings. Rules are rules."

"You're kidding me!" Britney protested.

Julia had been waiting for a moment like this all year. "What would this school be if we let people like you break the rules?"

Britney surprisingly didn't reply. Her eyes just wandered over Julia's shoulder to something behind her. Julia turned around to see what Britney was staring at. Coach was standing right there with her hands on her hips.

Julia felt dizzy. All the blood flowed out of Julia's face as she realized her own hypocrisy. Who was she to enforce the letter of the law? Who was she to be unmerciful?

"Britney!" Coach barked. "I guess you're late. Three seconds. Apparently today we need to follow the law down to the letter in this gym. So you're tardy. But as you get into line with your little tardiness, Julia and I need to take a little walk to the office to handle something else. After all, rules are rules."

She turned to Julia. "Sorry Julia, but by your own choosing, I guess mercy isn't being extended in this gym today. Not even for three seconds."

Coach didn't say another word. She just walked Julia to the vice principal's office and handed her over to Mr. Ramos. Julia confessed everything that happened. Even though she didn't actually smoke pot, she was suspended for "consorting with students who partook of drugs." It went on her permanent record and she lost her position as TA.

Worst of all, she lost the trust of her coach.

TRANSITION STATEMENT

Actually, this story is 2,000 years old. Sure, I added the part about the Sentra and the pot smoking, but the basic premise is the same as when Jesus told this story. The key to understanding why Jesus told this story is in the numbers. The three seconds in the story are significant. It's a comparison. Why are the numbers important?

APPLICATION AND SCRIPTURE

When Jesus told his story, it was in response to Peter's answer to his own question: "How many times do I have to forgive someone, seven?" Notice how Peter tried to answer his own question with what he thought was the answer. Peter had done his homework. In the Jewish tradition you would forgive someone three times, but not four. Peter thought he would be safe, doubling the three and then adding one more—seven.

Jesus answered Peter by basically saying, "No Peter, not seven but 70 times seven" or way more than you can count. In other words, don't put numerical limits on forgiveness.

Then Jesus told a story about forgiveness using some absurdly high numbers. He used 10,000 talents, which in Jesus' day represented the largest number used in everyday math. In the story Jesus told, a servant owed a king this huge amount and couldn't possibly pay it back. The servant begged the king, and surprisingly, the king forgave the whole debt. But then this just-forgiven servant saw a fellow servant who owed him a small amount of money, demanding that he pay back the entire amount. When this other servant begged for mercy, the king's servant didn't budge and threw his fellow servant in jail until the debt was paid in full. The king found out about his servant's hypocritical lack of mercy, and...well...I'll read exactly what happened in Matthew 18:

32"Then the master called the servant in. 'You wicked servant,' he said, 'I canceled all that debt of yours because you begged me to. 33Shouldn't you have had mercy on your fellow servant just as I had on you?' 34In anger his master handed him over to the jailers to be tortured, until he should pay back all he owed.

35"This is how my heavenly Father will treat each of you unless you forgive your brother or sister from your heart."

It's like this. God has forgiven us more than we can measure. There's nothing we can do to earn this forgiveness. At the same time, he won't tolerate us abusing his grace. As forgiven people, we need to be forgiving people.

Jesus says that there is a new math of grace and mercy that begins when we give to others the forgiveness that God has given to us.

God does not put limits on forgiveness. When you forgive someone, grace and mercy is added to your life exponentially...beyond measurements.

Julia did not really understand what it meant to forgive. She was only free to be in that position of power because her coach had forgiven her. But Julia used her power for personal gain over someone she hated. And Jesus said that God would not tolerate that kind of misuse of mercy, grace and power. There is no incongruity with God's magnanimous forgiveness and his righteous judgment. It is because God is so compassionate and merciful that he cannot and will not tolerate those who are not.

CLOSING

Forgiveness is a process. We have to work at forgiving because true forgiveness is humanly impossible. I don't want to forgive. It is too much about seeing the other person squirm the same way I have. It is too much about justice. "How do you who have caused me pain get off scot-free? I do not want to forgive." It's only by the grace of God that I see how much I have been forgiven and am able to forgive.

As we close in prayer, who do you need to forgive? Let's pause a minute and think about it. Ask God to help you forgive that person or persons and show mercy. It may not be going to them and saying, "I forgive you." It might just be a simple act like inviting them to your party or an evening with your friends. Including them might be the act of forgiveness that Jesus wants from you.

Let's pray.

SMALL GROUP QUESTIONS

1. **Around the Circle:** Share about a time when you could have gotten in big trouble, but instead you were forgiven.

2. **Ask Just a Few:** Why do you think Coach forgave Julia and Maddy in the first place?

3. **Ask Just a Few:** Why did she change her mind?

In the story Jesus told, a servant owed a king this huge amount and couldn't possibly pay it back. The servant begged the king, and surprisingly, the king forgave the whole debt. But then the servant saw a fellow servant that owed him a small amount of money, demanding that he pay back the entire amount. When this other servant begged for mercy, the king's servant didn't budge and threw his fellow servant in jail until the debt was paid in full. The king found out about his servant's hypocritical lack of mercy, and got really mad.

³²*"Then the master called the servant in. 'You wicked servant,' he said, 'I canceled all that debt of yours because you begged me to.* ³³*Shouldn't you have had mercy on your fellow servant just as I had on you?'* ³⁴*In anger his master handed him over to the jailers to be tortured, until he should pay back all he owed.*

³⁵*"This is how my heavenly Father will treat each of you unless you forgive your brother or sister from your heart." (Matthew 18:32-35)*

4. **Ask Just a Few:** Why did the king get so mad?

5. **Ask Just a Few:** Why would someone be willing to receive forgiveness, but not give it?

6. **Ask Just a Few:** God is willing to forgive us for anything we've done in the past. Is it unfair for him to expect us to forgive others? Explain.

7. **Around the Circle:** Think of someone that you might be holding a grudge against. How can you let God begin to help you take this huge step? What does that look like?

8. **Around the Circle:** What is something you can do this week to show "forgiveness" to this person? How can I, as your youth group leader, help you do that?

TALK 03

TITLE: KEEPING THE GOAL IN SIGHT... EVEN WHEN YOU CAN'T SEE IT

TOPICS: Focus on Christ, Faith

BIG IDEA: When the foggy circumstances of life cloud your vision, keep your eyes of faith on Jesus.

SCRIPTURE

> Therefore, since we are surrounded by such a great cloud of witnesses, let us throw off everything that hinders and the sin that so easily entangles. And let us run with perseverance the race marked out for us, [2]fixing our eyes on Jesus, the pioneer and perfecter of faith. For the joy set before him he endured the cross, scorning its shame, and sat down at the right hand of the throne of God. [3]Consider him who endured such opposition from sinners, so that you will not grow weary and lose heart. (Hebrews 12:1-3)

PARTICULARS

This is the true story of Florence Chadwick who swam the 23 miles of the English Channel, both ways, but failed to swim the 21 miles from

Catalina Island to the California coast because of the fog. This story has a powerful lesson about faith.

It has a good number of details to memorize, so you'll want to spend a little more time rehearsing this one than some of the others.

STORY

Do you know how many laps it would take in the typical high school pool if you wanted to swim a mile? Between 65 and 71 laps.

Anyone here ever swam a mile in a pool without stopping? That's quite an accomplishment.

But can you imagine swimming a mile in the ocean?

Pools are nice. You get to touch a wall every lap, you have lane lines to keep you on course, and you don't have to worry about sharks or jellyfish. In the ocean...not so much.

Now...anyone here ever swam 21 miles without stopping?

And in the ocean?

Most long-distance swimmers crank out between 60 and 70 strokes a minute. A 10-hour swim requires 42,000 strokes. A 15-hour swim would require 63,000 strokes. That's what 34-year-old Florence Chadwick was ready to do on July 4, 1952. She was going to swim 21 miles in the Pacific Ocean, from Catalina Island to the California shore, a feat no woman had ever accomplished.

Ocean swims bring up a whole new set of variables. Open-water swimmers who tackle ocean swims almost always encounter currents, waves, and wind. A swimmer attempting a 21-mile swim might actually swim several miles farther, depending on currents. Add to that many of the obstacles they might face: sharks, jellyfish, kelp beds, and oil fuel patches. Open-water competitors often emerge from the ocean swollen and scarred from jellyfish stings, sunburn, and swimsuit chafing.

But Florence Chadwick was used to enduring through these conditions. Her 21-mile swim on this foggy July day wouldn't be her first feat of this kind. She had been swimming long distances in open water her entire life.

Florence grew up on the beaches of San Diego, competing as a swimmer for the first time at age six when her uncle entered her in a race. As a young girl it was already evident that Florence had a knack for endurance races. She didn't care much for sprints—Florence loved distance!

At 11 years old, Florence won first place in a six-mile rough water race across the San Diego Bay Channel. This kid was probably one of the only 11-year-olds who would have survived an escape from Alcatraz!

At 13, Florence came in second at the U.S. national championships. For the next 20 years she competed in swimming events, thriving in any venue that offered long distance.

In 1936 she actually tried out for the U.S. Olympic team. She didn't qualify because all the events were short distances.

In 1950, Florence decided to tackle the greatest open-water swimming challenge at the time—the English Channel. The distance across the Channel was about 23 miles. Fewer than seven percent of those who attempt the swim actually complete it. On August 8, 1950, Florence not only made the swim from France to England, she beat the world record by over an hour, with a 13 hour and 20 minute swim. In an interview after the swim Florence said, "I feel fine. I am quite prepared to swim back."

Swimming back might not sound problematic for someone like Florence, but it proved to be a much more daunting task. No woman had ever swam the channel from England to France before, a much more difficult swim because of the winds and tides. But on a September morning in 1951, Florence finished the swim in a record time of 16 hours and 22 minutes.

So it would seem as though the 21-mile Catalina Island swim on July 4, 1952 shouldn't have been a problem. Florence had done greater distances and conquered more formidable challenges. She was prepared for sharks, jellyfish, currents, winds, and tides. She was in shape for the distance and motivated to be the first woman to accomplish it. But there was one element that Florence wasn't ready for...fog!

Californians who live on the coast are familiar with fog. When Florence got into the icy cold waters that morning and began the swim, the fog was so thick she couldn't even see the boats that followed her. It's a good thing Florence had support boats that day. Several times her support crew had to scare away sharks with rifles. But Florence wasn't worried about the sharks or any other elements. Her concern came every time she looked up to see her goal—the North American coast.

Nothing. She saw nothing but fog.

Florence swam for more than 15 hours while America watched on television. Her trainer and her mom encouraged her from one of the support boats. "Keep going! You're almost there!"

But every time Florence looked up...

Fog.

At 15 hours and 55 minutes Florence looked up one last time. As she scanned the water in front of her, desperate for a glimpse of her goal, she wrestled mentally, fighting to persevere, thinking about all that she had accomplished: She swam the English Channel both ways, she was the first woman to complete many of these swims, and she beat the men's record almost every time. Today would be yet another victory...if she could just see her destination.

But all she saw was fog.

Just before 16 hours, Florence asked her support boat to take her out of the water.

Florence gave up. It was the only time Florence Chadwick ever quit.

Florence was only a half a mile from the California coast when she gave up.

Why?

She couldn't see her goal.

As Florence sat on the beach, feeling the true agony of defeat, she told a reporter, "Look, I'm not excusing myself, but if I could have seen land I know I could have made it."

The fog had defeated her.

TRANSITION STATEMENT

Like Florence, many Christians lose heart because of the fog of life's circumstances. We can't see the purpose, the end, the goal, and the reason to keep going, and we are tempted to give up.

APPLICATION AND SCRIPTURE

What is some of the fog that has rolled into your life that hinders you from staying on course?

One of the more relevant questions that many of us might be asking is, "How do I stay on course when distractions blind me from the truth?"

The answer? Faith.

Yeah, I know. *Faith* is one of those words we use all the time in church. But in the book of Hebrews, the author actually defines it in chapter 11, giving us examples of people who lived a life of faith. Then the author tells us the secret to actually living it out in chapter 12, using the analogy of a race:

Therefore, since we are surrounded by such a great cloud of witnesses, let us throw off everything that hinders and the sin that so easily entangles. And let us run with perseverance the race marked out for us, ²fixing our eyes on Jesus, the pioneer and perfecter of faith. For the joy set before him he endured the cross, scorning its shame, and sat down at the right hand of the throne of God. ³Consider him who endured such opposition from sinners, so that you will not grow weary and lose heart. (Hebrews 12:1-3)

What does it look like to live a life of faith?

First, the author says, "throw off everything that hinders." A lot of us really fail at this. Some of us even welcome temptations that hinder. We flirt with influences that are fogging our thinking, and as a result we get "entangled," to use the word from the verse.

What kind of faith is this?

How are we being faithful when we flirt with the very temptations that God warns us to avoid? That's not putting our faith in God...that's giving in to our desires.

Well, this verse instructs us to throw those temptations away. Maybe that means deleting something on our iPods. Maybe that means literally unplugging something in our bedrooms. Maybe it means surrounding ourselves with people who encourage our faith, not distract us from it.

But then what?

It's nice that this passage doesn't just tell us what not to do...it tells us what to do. To encourage us to be faithful even when the foggy circumstances of life begin to destroy our faith, he tells us to fix our eyes on Jesus.

How much time are you spending with Jesus? It's a simple question. But in all honesty, how much time are you focusing on him, reading his teachings, practicing his example, and remembering the sacrifice that he paid for each one of us? Or as the verse put it, how often do we "consider him who endured such opposition from sinners, so that you will not grow weary and lose heart"?

Get rid of the sin that hinders.

Fix your eyes on Jesus.

On that foggy July morning, Florence might have lost that battle, but she returned to Catalina Island two months later to accomplish her goal. The fog was just as thick that day, but this time Florence swam with her faith intact. She knew her destination was there even if she couldn't see it. Florence completed the swim in 13 hours, 47 minutes and 55 seconds, not only becoming the first woman to accomplish the swim, but shattering the men's record by more than two hours!

She knew her destination was there, even though she couldn't see it. The author of Hebrews is telling us that all of these people in chapter 11 who endured times when God seemed so far away were people of faith. They knew their destination was to be with Jesus someday and experience joy with him. Even though they couldn't see him personally, they believed in him.

Source: Gale Encyclopedia of Biography: Florence Chadwick

CLOSING

As you think about Florence, the many Old Testament "winners" of Hebrews 11, and Jesus, pray with me that God will help you have the faith that Jesus is there, even though you can't see him.

Let's pray.

SMALL GROUP QUESTIONS

1. **Around the Circle:** What is the longest distance you've ever swam?

2. **Ask Just a Few:** Why did Florence stop swimming when she had only a half mile to go?

3. **Ask Just a Few:** What is some of the fog that rolls into people's lives today that hinders them from "staying on course"?

The author of Hebrews tells us some great advice in chapter 12:

Therefore, since we are surrounded by such a great cloud of witnesses, let us throw off everything that hinders and the sin that so easily entangles. And let us run with perseverance the race marked out for us, 2 fixing our eyes on Jesus, the pioneer and perfecter of faith. For the joy set before him he endured the cross, scorning its shame, and sat down at the right hand of the throne of God. (Hebrews 12:1-2)

4. **Ask Just a Few:** What does he tell us to throw off?

5. **Around the Circle:** What could be some of these things hindering us that we need to throw off?

6. **Ask Just a Few:** What does the verse tell us to fix our eyes on? How do we do that?

7. **Around the Circle:** What is one way we can try to focus on Christ this week? How can I, as your youth group leader, help you do that?

TALK 04
TITLE: FROM GOALS TO WELLS

TOPICS: Vision, Gifts, Giving

BIG IDEA: Jesus can use "what we have" to make an impact.

SCRIPTURE

> [15]As evening approached, the disciples came to him and said, "This is a remote place, and it's already getting late. Send the crowds away, so they can go to the villages and buy themselves some food."
>
> [16]Jesus replied, "They do not need to go away. You give them something to eat." (Matthew 14:15-16)

PARTICULARS

This true story is the account of a young woman in our church who decided to tackle a national crisis. Rather than being overwhelmed by the problem, she used "what she had," her passion for soccer, to do something about it. Olivia and her ministry (fq2w.org) challenge all of us.

STORY

Olivia Hinkle was sitting in church, and she was getting bored. As her 19-year-old mind began to wander, she was thinking about her passion—soccer. She played all the time and wondered if she could somehow glorify God by playing soccer. After all, she was in church and she did love God. Could she somehow use her gift as a soccer player for the glory of God?

As she started brainstorming, she recalled hearing about a friend who did a bowl-a-thon. Olivia didn't bowl, but she figured if people raise money through bowling, why couldn't she raise money through soccer?

She didn't know what this would look like, but she figured it was something she would have to eventually try.

While a student in college, Olivia traveled to Uganda in Africa and was overwhelmed by the need for drinkable water. Every day the people of rural Uganda travel to polluted springs for the water they use to drink, cook, and wash their clothes. These springs are the same springs where animals drink, bathe, and even relieve themselves. Dysentery and diarrhea, the top causes of death among Ugandan children, run rampant because they consume this unclean water.

As she thought about her love for soccer and the need for drinkable water in Africa, an idea began to take root in her mind. Could she use soccer to get money for drilling wells so that obtaining clean, drinkable water would become as easy as turning on a faucet? She began to imagine the possibilities. Could she get corporate and individual sponsorships? Could she put together a team that would play to raise money? Could she raise money by the number of goals scored or for each win?

How could a young college student fulfill her dream?

When Olivia graduated from college, she combined her three passions to make it happen. She had a passion for God, a passion for soccer, and a passion for the people in Uganda who desperately needed clean water. So Olivia started a nonprofit called "From Goals to Wells."

Since soccer camps are huge for young players, Olivia decided to create a soccer camp for 12-to-15-year-olds. Olivia's idea was to use all the profits from the camp to raise the $1,500 to install a water-filtration wall in a Ugandan village. As water travels through these walls, it is filtered and decontaminated and fresh water is dispensed.

Olivia had played soccer at Concordia University in southern California and had tons of contacts with expert, highly competitive players. Olivia recruited many of these players as coaches. But this was not your typical soccer camp. In addition to focusing on skills, techniques, and team strategies, Olivia took time each day to instruct the campers about the water issues in Uganda and taught them about the country. As a result of attending this camp, the participants walked away not only with improved soccer skills but also with the understanding and knowledge that they were making a difference in the lives of the people of Uganda.

Unfortunately, her first camp only had 30 participants, and she didn't reach her goal. But that didn't stop Olivia. She challenged a church to help her raise the funds with their vacation Bible school program—and they did. Together they raised the $1,500 to build the water-filtration wall in Uganda.

Olivia's "Goals to Wells" was off and running. She sent the $1,500 for the water-filtration wall to Assist International, an organization that specializes in providing water-filtration walls made of gravel and rock.

But the story isn't over.

A year later Olivia went on another Ugandan trip with a team from her church. She convinced the mission team to take the two-hour drive on rural roads to northern Uganda to see the well. The team stopped at an orphanage to find directions, and then they traveled over rough, dirt roads in the middle of nowhere. Soon they came upon the well.

Olivia leapt from the vehicle and ran over to the well. It didn't look like much, but it was fresh water. Tears filled her eyes.

As the California team gathered around the well and witnessed the tears in Olivia's eyes, something happened. A few Ugandan women and children showed up at the well with huge water containers on their heads to get water and wondered whom these white people were standing around their well. The African pastor traveling with the team explained to the women that Olivia had raised the money and made arrangements to have the well placed there, and immediately the women burst into songs and started praising God. They sang, clapped, danced, and started a long, wavering, high-pitched trilling sound called an *ululation*.

Olivia wept with joy.

Olivia was just a soccer player with a dream. And her daydream in church that morning would continue to provide clean water for 2,000 people in that one well alone for 10 to 15 years.

Olivia's second camp had more than 50 participants, and she met her goal of $1,500 for another well. Ask Olivia. This is just the start.

TRANSITION STATEMENT

Do you often feel overwhelmed when you hear about the problems in the world? What can I do about the world problems of poverty, hunger, sicknesses, injustice, and clean water? Maybe you're like Olivia and you want to help, but you wonder how? After all, I'm just one person and I don't have the resources to even make a dent in the problem.

Olivia reflects that when she was very young she always felt, "What can I do? I'm not a doctor, or a preacher, or a musician. I'm just a soccer player."

APPLICATION AND SCRIPTURE

There is great news. Jesus can use "whatever we have" to make an impact.

In the New Testament there is a story that is repeated four times. God must want us to get the point of how the disciples were overwhelmed, but Jesus wanted to change their perspective. They saw the situation as a huge problem and felt that they could not do anything about it. But Jesus did not see it that way.

Listen to the story and see if you can observe just how differently the disciples and Jesus see the problem in Matthew 14:13-21:

[13]When Jesus heard what had happened, he withdrew by boat privately to a solitary place. Hearing of this, the crowds followed him on foot from the towns. [14]When Jesus landed and saw a large crowd, he had compassion on them and healed their sick.

[15]As evening approached, the disciples came to him and said, "This is a remote place, and it's already getting late. Send the crowds away, so they can go to the villages and buy themselves some food."

[16]Jesus replied, "They do not need to go away. You give them something to eat."

[17]"We have here only five loaves of bread and two fish," they answered.

[18]"Bring them here to me," he said. [19]And he directed the people to sit down on the grass. Taking the five loaves and the two fish and looking up to heaven, he gave thanks and broke the loaves. Then he gave them to the disciples, and the disciples gave them to the people. [20]They all ate and were

satisfied, and the disciples picked up twelve basketfuls of broken pieces that were left over. [21]The number of those who ate was about five thousand men, besides women and children.

The story is about feeding the 5,000 men, plus women and children. There could have been 10,000 to 20,000 hungry people, and the disciples said to Jesus, "Send them away so they can get something to eat."

The huge numbers overwhelmed the disciples. But Jesus told them, "No, don't send them away, get them something to eat." (v. 16) He put the problem back on them.

The disciples found five loaves and two fish (v. 17). Jesus asked the disciples to bring the food to him, and when they did, Jesus took the five loaves and two fish and performed a miracle. He prayed over the available food, blessed it, and started handing it out to the hungry people.

Jesus didn't ask the disciples to perform a miracle. He only asked the disciples to bring what they had found. Then Jesus performed the miracle. That is all Jesus asks of us.

It is easy for us to become overwhelmed by these facts:

- Less than 1 percent of the world's fresh water is readily accessible.

- Every 20 seconds a child dies from a water-related disease.

- About 80 percent of sewage in developing countries is discharged untreated.

- More people have cell phones than access to a decent toilet.

- 3.6 million people die each year from a water-related disease.

- Nearly 1 billion people lack access to safe water.

- Millions of women and children spend several hours a day collecting water from distant, often polluted sources.

Jesus doesn't want us to be overwhelmed, but he doesn't want us to ignore it either. He wants us to bring him what we have.

Olivia gave what she had. She was not overwhelmed by the problem. She was burdened by it but did not say, "I have so little, I can't do much." No, she dreamed, "Hey, I love soccer, I can lead and organize, I have contacts with great players, and we can work together to raise money for wells." That is all Jesus asks. He does not ask us to give what we don't have. He only asks us to give what we have and do what we can.

CLOSING

As we close, think about what gifts God has given to you. Do you have leadership gifts? Do you have a passion for something like Olivia did such as soccer? Is there a way that you can glorify God with that passion?

I challenge you to begin to pray this prayer, "God, how can I glorify you with the gifts and abilities that you have given to me in light of the needs I see?" And be prepared for God to perform the miracle in your life like he did for Olivia.

Let's pray.

SMALL GROUP QUESTIONS

1. **Around the Circle:** Olivia was daydreaming in church one day and came up with this idea. What do you do when you are bored in church?

2. **Ask Just a Few:** Olivia really wanted to make a difference, but she didn't know how. Can anyone relate to that? What ideas did you come up with?

3. **Around the Circle:** When Olivia saw the huge need for water in Uganda, her heart broke. She wanted to help. Share if you've ever seen a need and wanted to help. Did you do anything?

Jesus demonstrated that we don't need to be overwhelmed by these huge world problems. Instead, we can give what we have.

In the Scripture we just heard, literally thousands of people were hungry. The disciples found five loaves and two fish. Jesus asked the disciples to bring the food to him, and Jesus took the five loaves and two fish and performed a miracle. He prayed over the food available, blessed it, and started handing it out to the thousands of hungry people.

Olivia didn't become overwhelmed with the problem of bad water in Uganda. Instead she saw the opportunity to build a well. That opportunity led to another. Because of that, thousands of people now have clean water.

4. **Ask Just a Few:** What did Olivia have to offer to God?

5. **Ask Just a Few:** How did God use Olivia's talents and abilities?

6. **Around the Circle:** What gifts do you have that God might be able to use? How could you use those gifts to make an impact?

7. **Around the Circle:** What's one thing you can do this week to pursue this? How can I, as your youth group leader, help you do that?

TALK 05
TITLE: FIVE CHOICES AGO

TOPICS: Temptation, Sin

BIG IDEA: The destructive path of sin begins with one choice that sets us up for failure.

SCRIPTURE

> [13]When tempted, no one should say, "God is tempting me." For God cannot be tempted by evil, nor does he tempt anyone; [14]but each person is tempted when they are dragged away by their own evil desire and enticed. [15]Then, after desire has conceived, it gives birth to sin; and sin, when it is full-grown, gives birth to death.
> (James 1:13-15)

PARTICULARS

This story is about how we often set ourselves up for failure because we underestimate the power of our vulnerabilities. We all have them. Chris' problem was alcohol. We each have areas where we are vulnerable, and we soon are too far down the path to turn back. So many of us do that all the time.

STORY

As Chris drove his rusted 1994 Plymouth down Main Avenue, he saw that familiar street sign ahead.

Central Ave.

The left-turn lane was empty, and the light was green. It would be so easy to just turn left...but deep inside, Chris knew what that would mean.

That turn lane probably didn't mean much to most people, but to Chris it meant a turn down a dark corridor of his life that he'd rather not revisit.

Chris never wanted to be an alcoholic, but who does? Five years prior, Chris' choices had taken him down a broad downhill slope where his entire existence became wrapped around the bottle. His addiction eventually cost him his marriage, his job, and his driver's license. It was only at this point—rock bottom—that Chris realized, *I need help.*

After several attempts at various 12-step programs, Chris finally found a circle of people meeting in the basement of an old Methodist church who helped him get a grip on his addiction. Chris was now three months sober, had his license back, and a job working for an auto body shop owned by one of his new friends from the program.

But at this moment, driving home from work this particular day, Chris was completely alone in his car.

As Chris saw the turn lane, he began to reminisce. He selectively remembered the fun times he used to have with Troy, Brian and Sean at O'Malley's Bar. Chris hadn't been to O'Malley's since...well, it had been a long time.

Chris could almost feel the "three months" chip burning a hole in the front right pocket of his work pants. This small token from his AA meeting represented the victories of numerous small battles in a self-inflicted war that Chris would fight for the rest of his life.

As Chris approached the all-too-familiar left-turn lane on Central, another battle was being fought in his head.

It's been so long since I've even driven down this street, Chris thought. *I don't want a drink, I'm just curious if O'Malley's is even still in business. For all I know, it's closed.*

Chris steered into the left-turn lane.

I'll just drive by. I'm not going to stop—I'm just curious if the bar is still there.

As Chris turned left, he took a deep breath. His thoughts were telling him nothing was going to happen, but his breathing and every other sense in his body seemed to know better.

I'm just going to drive by, Chris assured himself.

It wasn't but a minute before Chris saw that old familiar sign in front of O'Malley's. "Friends and Spirits."

As soon as the bar was in sight, Chris began to ponder. *I wonder if Brian, Troy, and Sean are there?*

His mind flashed with memories of the four of them sitting in the corner booth, talking, laughing, and calling Nikki over for another refill. The sound of the glass being filled. The sweet aroma.

Chris slowed down to peer into the parking lot. *I just wonder if those guys are here today. I'm not going in. I'm just curious if they still even visit O'Malley's.*

Chris was tempted to turn left into the driveway. His hands fought the decision, almost as if they knew the ramifications, but Chris's justifications were quick. *I'm just going to pull in and see if I spot their cars—just for curiosity's sake.*

Chris turned left into the parking lot and quickly spotted Brian's blue Chevy, and Sean's Honda.

They're here, Chris told himself. *Now you can go on your way.*

Chris pulled his car into a spot to turn around, placed his hand on the shifter...and paused.

Just put the car in reverse, pull out, and go on your way.

That was one thought. But another thought was entering his head: *I haven't seen these guys in over a year. They must think I'm a jerk. No calls, no explanation...just complete seclusion.*

His rationalization gained momentum: *I'm a jerk. I can't treat people like that. I need to at least say "Hi."*

Something in Chris knew the ramifications of what he was contemplating, but Chris was quick to retort. *I'm not going to drink. I'm just going to pop in and say "Hi." It's the right thing to do.*

Chris looked down at his hands. They were shaking. He couldn't even tell why. It was almost as if they were excited. The hairs on his arms were standing straight up.

Chris left his car. A moment later he was in the threshold of the bar's front door, gazing around the room. His eyes immediately floated to the corner booth. Sure enough, Brian and Sean were there. Before Chris could even speak, Brian caught sight of him.

"No way! Chris! Is that really you?"

Sean turned and connected eyes with Chris as well.

"I can't believe it!" Sean stole a swig from his glass, wiping his lips with the back of his hand. "Get over here."

With his hands in his pockets, Chris walked over to the table. Brian and Sean stood up to greet Chris, exchanging hugs.

"I'm not here to drink," Chris quickly pronounced. He held up his three-month pin proudly.

Brian and Sean were silent for a few seconds. Finally Brian broke the silence. "Well sure," he said, patting Chris on the shoulder. "Let's order you a club soda then."

Sean turned toward the bar. "Nikki! A club soda over here!"

Chris sat with his friends for a few minutes, catching up on old times. It had been a year. Brian had a new girlfriend. Sean had a new hunting dog. Both were named Rosy. That was good for at least five minutes of laughter.

And that's when Sean did it. He stared Chris in the eyes for a moment, tilting his head slightly like he was trying to figure him out. "Come on, man. Who ya fooling here? We know why you're here...and it ain't for club soda."

Chris didn't know what to say. He glanced over at Brian. Brian looked down and rubbed his forefinger across the top of his glass.

"Nikki!" Sean barked. "A Jim Beam for my man Chris over here."

Chris started to object, but Sean held out his hand. "I got this!"

Nikki brought over a shot glass filled with that all-too-familiar drink and set it in front of Chris—who just stared at the glass. He could smell it, even though his nose was probably a good 18 inches from the glass. He closed his eyes, but that only helped him remember the feeling of the pleasant solution passing over his tongue and warming his throat as it went down.

Chris lifted the glass to his lips and inhaled the recognizable scent coming from the small glass.

Why? he asked himself. *Why is this so difficult? Why is this so hard to resist? Who could resist this temptation?*

TRANSITION STATEMENT

Who could resist that temptation? Think about this for a moment. You're an alcoholic. You're sitting in a bar with friends. You've got your favorite drink in front of you, you've lifted it to your lips, and you're taking in the aroma.

Who could possibly resist this?

But Chris's problem isn't learning how to fight this kind of temptation. Chris's problem is that he set himself up for failure.

So many of us do that all the time!

APPLICATION AND SCRIPTURE

The New Testament writer, James, understood this process when he wrote in chapter one of his book:

[13]When tempted, no one should say, "God is tempting me." For God cannot be tempted by evil, nor does he tempt anyone; [14]but each person is tempted when they are dragged away by their own evil desire and enticed. [15]Then, after desire has conceived, it gives birth to sin; and sin, when it is full-grown, gives birth to death. (James 1:13-15)

Notice the steps to sin. It all starts with desire. Our direction is determined by what captures our attention, our desires. James says that

God does not tempt us. He loves us too much to do that. So where does temptation come from? It comes from our inward desires, a basic emptiness we want to fill.

Chris's mistake wasn't just lifting a glass to his lips—it was long before then. It began with that left turn which resulted in sitting down in the booth with his drinking buddies. The steps to failure were walking into a bar, getting out of his car, and pulling into the parking lot. But it all began with turning left on Central Avenue. He probably thought like many of us, *I try and try not to yield, I pray, and I keep vowing; I'm tired of being tricked by temptation. Why?*

James conveys that it's because of deception. We deceive ourselves into thinking, "I can handle this." But we can't. Paul in Romans 7:19 says, "For I do not do the good I want to do, but the evil I do not want to do—this I keep on doing." Once we make that left turn, like Chris did, we are on the path of deception. James says that we deceive ourselves. Chris deceived himself with these kinds of thoughts:

- *I'm just going to pull in and see if I spot their cars—just for curiosity's sake.*
- His mind flashed with memories of the four of them sitting in the corner booth, talking, laughing, and calling Nikki over for another refill. The sound of the glass being filled. The aroma.
- Chris slowed down to peer into the parking lot. *I just wonder if those guys are here today? I'm not going in. I'm just curious if they still even visit O'Malley's.*

Chris is on the path of destruction because he is thinking about his desires—old desires that never will go away.

Then James uses a strong word—*enticed.* Or in some translations, *bait.* In fishing, the bait is made to hide the hook. It looks great. That's the word James uses. It is the lure of pleasure. We are so deceived that we don't understand we are being sucked in.

As Chris thought about his friends he hadn't seen in a while, he began to worry about what they must think of him, so in his rationalization he took the bait and turned off the car. Something in Chris knew the ramifications of what he was contemplating, but Chris was quick to retort: *I'm not going to drink. I'm just going to pop in and say "Hi." It's the right thing to do.*

Which James would call the next logical and seductive step—action. The bait was set and he took the bite. It was just a club soda with old friends. Chris even announced that he had not had a drink for three months. But one of his friends, Sean, put it to Chris straight when he said, "Come on, man. Who ya fooling here? We know why you're here... and it ain't for club soda."

Chris didn't know how to respond. He had taken the bait. The hook was set.

"Nikki!" Sean barked. "A Jim Beam for my man Chris over here."

And James describes what happens next as the pain of death. When temptation is full grown, it produces the pain of consequences. The kicks of the moment have kickbacks. We want to be free, to have the freedom of choice. And God has given us that choice. But we don't have the freedom to pick the consequences.

John Owen wrote in the 1600s what sums up Chris' experience—and what Owen describes when he writes, "Temptations and occasions put nothing into a man, but only draw out what was in him before."

The God who cannot be tempted (because there is no sin within him that responds to temptation) does not tempt, either. Temptation comes from within us. It begins with desire, and when this desire is facilitated, the fruit it bears is sin. And sin results in death. Sin and death are the result of a sequence of events, all of which begin with a desire which is not of God and isn't rejected and resisted.

CLOSING

What are the "left turns" in your life you need to avoid? Once you make the first left turn, like Chris did, each turn after that takes you down the road of deception, bait, action, and finally consequences.

Let's bow our heads and close our eyes to pray. And before we do, some of you might be thinking about a left turn in your life right now. There's no better time to deal with it than right now. As everyone's eyes are closed and heads are bowed, I want to encourage you to do something. If you would like to deal with that temptation right now, we'd love to help. One of the adults in the room would love to talk with you about it, offering you encouragement and help. All you need to do is raise your hand right now. By putting your hand up, you're saying, "I wanna talk about this." After I pray and we dismiss, walk up to one of the leaders and simply say, "I raised my hand."

Let's pray.

SMALL GROUP QUESTIONS

1. **Around the Circle:** What is your favorite food or drink?

2. **Ask Just a Few:** How did Chris' problem begin that day?

3. **Ask Just a Few:** Why was turning left on Central Avenue a bad idea?

4. **Ask Just a Few:** Is it difficult for an alcoholic to resist a drink, in a bar, with friends, when it's just under his nose? Then why do we do that with other temptations in our lives?

James talks about temptations in the passage we just heard:

> [13]When tempted, no one should say, "God is tempting me." For God cannot be tempted by evil, nor does he tempt anyone; [14]but each person is tempted when they are dragged away by their own evil desire and enticed. [15]Then, after desire has conceived, it gives birth to sin; and sin, when it is full-grown, gives birth to death. (James 1:13-15)

5. **Ask Just a Few:** The passage says that temptations don't come from God. Where do they come from (v. 14)?

6. **Ask Just a Few:** The passage says that these temptations from our own desires "entice" us or "bait" us. How?

7. **Ask Just a Few:** What are some of the common temptations or desires that entice teenagers and drag us away?

8. **Ask Just a Few:** How do we sometimes make that first "left turn" toward some of these temptations?

9. **Ask Just a Few:** What does the passage say happens when we allow this sin to grow in us? (v. 15)

10. **Around the Circle:** What is a left turn that we need to avoid this week? How can I, as your youth group leader, help you do that?

TALK 06
TITLE: I DON'T BELONG

TOPICS: Reaching Out to Others, Evangelism

BIG IDEA: We can make a huge impact when we leave our comfort zones and take the long journey to meet people where they are.

SCRIPTURE

> The brothers and sisters there had heard that we were coming, and they traveled as far as the Forum of Appius and the Three Taverns to meet us. At the sight of these people Paul thanked God and was encouraged.
> (Acts 28:15)

PARTICULARS

This is based on a true story about a student that my friend Mark Oestreicher knew. When I heard Mark tell the story, I knew it would have a profound impact on others, so I asked his permission to use it for this book. He has also included part of this story in his book, *A Beautiful Mess*.

STORY

Michael was a typical middle school kid who attended a big church with his family. He wasn't the most popular kid, he wasn't super outgoing... and he wasn't perfect.

Michael really enjoyed the junior high group, but like most kids he wanted to be noticed. It's not like Michael had a self-esteem issue; he just wished that someone knew his name, something that's a little more difficult in larger groups.

No one else at Michael's school went to the church, so there was a fairly natural disconnect from his life at school and his life at church. But Michael kept attending the youth group every week, looking for ways to connect. Slowly Michael started making friends in the group.

The adult leaders began getting to know Michael as well. In fact, one week the youth pastor invited Michael and two other middle school guys to be part of a discipleship group. Basically the three guys would each do devotionals on their own, then all three would get together with the youth pastor weekly. Michael really liked this time. He was committed to doing the devotionals each week and enjoyed talking about where his faith blended with real life.

Michael finally felt accepted at youth group. He was plugged in, he was growing in his faith...people knew his name.

Michael entered high school, and the switch to the high school group at the church wasn't a smooth one. The church was in the middle of transition, and an intern was running the high school ministry. The high school group was a completely different experience for Michael. The two middle school guys who he'd gotten to know through the discipleship group were younger and therefore didn't graduate yet to the high school group. So again, no one knew him—and no one made an effort to connect with him at all.

It was in the middle of this perfect storm of events that it happened.

Michael had a bad skateboard accident and became completely incapacitated for three months. During this time, no students from the church group ever reached out to him. They didn't visit, they didn't call, they didn't even text. A couple leaders visited him...but no one his own age.

Michael was really hurt. As he lay at home, he began to reflect on his entire church experience. The junior high ministry was a great experience, but the high school group was a completely different story. The upperclassmen made the freshmen feel like rejects from day one. No one had ever made an effort to talk with Michael. And Michael had tried. He went to some activities and had learned many of the other students' names. But other than, "Hey freshman...toss me that dodge ball!" no one talked with him much.

And now that he was home, incapacitated in bed, it was like no one even noticed he was gone.

After three months of recovering, Michael finally returned to school, and on Sunday he walked back into that familiar high school youth room. No one greeted him, so he just made his way to the back and sat down. As he sat in a chair by himself, he watched as groups of teenagers were laughing and talking with each other; but no one talked with Michael.

Nobody asked where he'd been.

No one told him, "We missed you Michael!"

Nothing.

A switch flipped in Michael's head. "I don't belong here."

And he never went back.

His mom and dad urged him to go, but 14-year-old Michael always made excuses. His parents didn't want to force him, so Michael began doing his own thing.

During this time Michael didn't have anything against God, he just didn't have any interest in going to church. His anger grew to a calcified belief that the church was a joke and nothing more than a gathering place for hypocrites.

Michael began spending a lot more time skateboarding. After school you would find Michael either riding or working on skateboards. He couldn't get enough.

Michael was a really intelligent kid. The monotony of school started to bore him. It just wasn't very challenging for him, so he dropped out, easily getting his GED instead and graduating early. Before long he took some entrepreneurial initiative and started his own skateboard shop in his hometown. The shop did well for a while, but the economy buckled, and he eventually had to close down.

Feeling the failure of his business and unsure about the future, Michael began toying with some destructive habits, experimenting with drinking and drugs. Michael was looking for anything to numb the pain.

But Michael wasn't defeated. Eventually he found an accounting job in another city. It wasn't his dream job, but it was work. Michael drifted through life, living day to day. During this time he never dropped his belief in God. He knew God was there, waiting for him, but Michael was too mad to return to church.

As the years passed, Michael rose through the ranks and became a manager at work. But he knew there was more to life. He began feeling the pull to try out a local church that he had been hearing about from some friends. Michael resisted at first, but eventually he gave in.

It would be nice to say that Michael returned to church because he was responding to God's prompting. But actually Michael's main motivation for giving church a try was to prove to himself that the church was full of phonies who would reject him once again.

By this time in life, Michael had full tattoos up and down his arms. Michael purposely wore a sleeveless shirt as he got dressed that morning before church as a "dare" to anyone who might cast him a judgmental glance.

As Michael arrived and walked across the parking lot, he prepared himself for the negative response he would receive; but the first person he encountered said, "Great tats, man. Who does your work?"

That was it. Michael was back.

Michael got plugged back in immediately, began growing in his faith once again, and now helps out in youth ministry today.

TRANSITION STATEMENT

Michael, like all of us, had a need to belong. The mission of the church is to fulfill that need in everybody. It didn't take much for Michael to feel like he was back. One person accepted him as he was—tattoos, fearful, and questioning.

There is a very interesting episode in the Apostle Paul's life that Luke chooses to record at the very end of the book of Acts. It must have meant something to Luke to be accepted so warmly by the church in Rome. They were at a point of need in their lives, and this incident touched him so much that he included it in his account of the book of Acts. Luke ends the episode basically saying, "We all took courage."

What was this action that encouraged Paul and Luke so much?

APPLICATION AND SCRIPTURE

The traveling group which included Paul and Luke had been ship-wrecked. They had spent the winter on an island, and in Acts 28:11-15, Luke talks about their journey, their stops, and the people that came out to greet them:

[11]After three months we put out to sea in a ship that had wintered in the island—it was an Alexandrian ship with the figurehead of the twin gods Castor and Pollux. [12]We put in at Syracuse and stayed there three days. [13]From there we set sail and arrived at Rhegium. The next day the south wind came up, and on the following day we reached Puteoli. [14]There we found some brothers and sisters who invited us to spend a week with them. And so we came to Rome. [15]The brothers and sisters there had heard that we were coming, and they traveled as far as the Forum of Appius and the Three Taverns to meet us. At the sight of these people Paul thanked God and was encouraged.

In verse 15 Luke describes how the church stepped up to meet the Apostle Paul and Luke's need to belong. The Bible says that the Roman Christians came to meet them. What we don't see in this casual reading is just what that trip was. Some walked the 43 miles to the Forum of Appius (back then they couldn't just hop in their cars), a sort of ancient "rest stop." Others walked 33 miles to the Three Taverns rest stop.

But what is significant about this story is that Luke mentions it. The kindness of those Christians to welcome Paul and Luke, to meet them where they were, is something Luke wants us to know. Some versions even interpret this last verse as "and we all took courage." This act inspired them. People making an effort to greet them made all the difference.

If even great men of faith like the Apostle Paul and Luke need to be encouraged, what about Michael? What about us?

That is what the church is to be when we are being the church.

We can make a huge impact when we leave our comfort zones and take the long journey to meet people where they are.

This is especially true in youth groups. Often we tend to hang out with our own friends—in our own comfort zones—and neglect the Michaels who are at difficult times in their lives. But you are better than this. I have watched some of you reach out to others in our group when they are hurting. You have traveled the distance and brought hope to others who enter these doors. I have also watched many of you reach out to the new Michaels who come to our youth meeting alone.

But unfortunately there are times we fail to leave our comfort zones to reach out. Could there be Michaels in our group right now? What message are we communicating to them?

Think about when you entered these doors for the first time. Many of you came into this group with your friends when you graduated from the eighth grade. Even though you may have had some fear, at least you had someone coming with you. But some of you had never been to this group before. You were alone. Do you remember what it was like? Like Michael, you also felt alone and fearful.

One small effort can make all the difference. Michael was at a vulnerable point, and one man stepped up. His actions and words said, "You are not alone here. You belong."

And Michael was back.

There are times after a long journey when I needed someone to walk with me the rest of the way. I thank God that at some tired times in my life, though I was still on the road to discipleship, there were brothers and sisters in Christ who left their places of comfort and met me at the Forum of Appius and the Three Taverns. I was encouraged when I saw them.

CLOSING

I pray that we will reach out. I pray that we would be the youth group that meets others' needs, wherever they are in their journeys. I pray that we develop a reputation like the church in Rome that cares enough to leave our comfort zones and extend a welcome in Jesus' name. That is what the church should be.

Let's pray.

SMALL GROUP QUESTIONS

1. **Around the Circle:** Describe a time when you felt alone or rejected by others.

2. **Ask Just a Few:** When Michael went to the high school group at the church, what were some of the circumstances that led to him feeling rejected?

3. **Ask Just a Few:** What could have the group done to make Michael feel more accepted?

In this interesting little passage in the book of Acts, we see some believers from Rome make a gesture to greet Paul and Luke:

The brothers and sisters there had heard that we were coming, and they traveled as far as the Forum of Appius and the Three Taverns to meet us. At the sight of these people Paul thanked God and was encouraged.

4. **Ask Just a Few:** What did the people of Rome do that encouraged Paul?

5. **Ask Just a Few:** How did Paul respond?

6. **Ask Just a Few:** In the story about Michael, what "small" gesture made Michael feel welcome after so many years? Why do you think such a small act helped?

7. **Ask Just a Few:** What are ways that we, as a church today, can work hard at encouraging others and making them feel accepted?

8. **Around the Circle:** Think about someone you might have seen sitting alone or perhaps feeling rejected at church or youth group. What's one action you can take the next time you see this person to make him or her feel accepted? How can I, as your youth group leader, help you do this?

TALK 07

TITLE: JETHRO

TOPIC: Dealing with Hardships

BIG IDEA: When God gives we ought to praise God for the inspiration, and when he takes away we ought to praise God for the memory.

SCRIPTURE

> ^{20}At this, Job got up and tore his robe and shaved his head. Then he fell to the ground in worship 21 and said:
>
> "Naked I came from my mother's womb,
> and naked I will depart.
> The Lord gave and the Lord has taken away;
> may the name of the Lord be praised." (Job 1:20-21)

PARTICULARS

This is a true story and I know it well because this is my family. It was a tough time for all of us, especially my daughter Ashley. I wrote it in the third person about my wife and Ashley so you can all tell the story.

Two ways you should NOT use this story:

1. I would not use this story after the death of a person, especially a really difficult situation like a suicide or accidental death.

You don't want to compare the death of an animal to the death of a human.

2. Please don't use this story to stir up the emotions of young people and then do an altar call. That's not the story's intention and would be a misuse of it. I don't believe in emotionalism as a tool.

I've used this story as a great tool to talk about how when God gives we ought to praise God for the inspiration, and when he takes away we ought to praise God for the memory.

STORY

It seemed like a normal Monday as Lori poured coffee in her favorite "to go" mug and hurried to the car, but the morning would prove to be anything but normal.

After dropping off Ashley, her 14-year-old daughter, at high school, Lori went home and loaded up their 105-pound Bernese Mountain Dog into the back of their SUV and headed to the vet.

Bernese Mountain Dogs, often called "Berners," are beautiful black dogs with white and brown on the face, a white chest and often a white tip on the tail. Some say they look like a mix between a Saint Bernard and a black lab. They're big, furry, and snuggly. Those are probably the adjectives that Lori and her family would have used to describe Jethro— emphasis on the snuggly part. Jethro excelled at being snuggly. This was a positive attribute if you were feeling down, depressed, and wanted a companion. It was a negative, however, if you didn't like a 105-pound drooling dog constantly trying to crawl onto your lap.

Jethro stuck his big head out the back passenger side window as Lori cruised down Greenback Lane toward the vet clinic. A "routine visit."

If only.

Jethro had become part of the family five years before. He was an impulse buy, a perfect example of why you should never take your kids to "just look" at puppies. Ashley, who was nine at the time, was obsessed with Bernese Mountain Dogs. Lori and her husband had never even heard of the breed, but little Ashley had bought books about them, stuffed animals, calendars...you name it. Being adventurous parents (or stupid parents—you decide), Lori and her husband decided it would be fun to visit a breeder and "just look."

Yeah, right.

Next thing you know, they brought Jethro home.

Jethro wasn't the most intelligent animal. He was big, klutzy, and nervous when he got in tight places. This combination of qualities wasn't a good mix when you happen to be walking through a doorway at the same time as Jethro. This dog was a knee injury waiting to happen.

Walking Jethro always was an experience as well. Lori's first run with the dog resulted in him getting spooked, flanking her, knocking her to the ground, and giving her a scar that she still has today. He was much better now, but he still outweighed Ashley, which could make him difficult to control if he wanted to go left when she wanted to go right.

Lori's family never owned a dog of great size before, so they never fathomed how much food the dog would consume...and eventually discharge from his body! We're talking serious dino-doo-doo! Add to this the fact that he always managed to stop and squat in the middle of an intersection whenever Lori would walk him. No one seemed to know why Jethro did this; perhaps he just preferred doing his business in wide open places. But guaranteed, anytime the family walked Jethro, he would do his business in the middle of an intersection. It's pretty embarrassing when your dog is building a miniature log cabin in the middle of a four-way stop while you're pulling out a 40-gallon plastic baggie for cleanup!

Despite these drawbacks, Jethro was always cheery with his tail wagging and a big goofy grin on his face. It didn't matter what kind of day you were having, Jethro wanted to be with you, snuggle up next to you, lay his monstrous head on your lap, and just love you.

Lori would always remember a particular day when Ashley was 13years old and Jethro was driving everyone crazy...everyone but Ashley. Ashley always had a tolerance for Jethro that no one else did. It's almost as if Ashley saw something in Jethro.

It was on this day that Ashley said something that Lori never forgot. Jethro had just noticeably frustrated Lori, lying down like a beached elephant seal resting between the dishwasher and the table, perfectly "in the way." Lori mumbled to herself, "Jethro, why do you always have to be right next to us!"

Overhearing Lori's comment, Ashley said, "I like that about Jethro. I find him inspiring!"

The rest of the family, who happened to be gathered in the kitchen at the time, all laughed. "What on earth is inspiring about this big doofus?"

"He's always happy," Ashley affirmed. "Even when life stinks, Jethro is content."

Ashley went on, "There's no drama with Jethro. He doesn't hold grudges, he doesn't play favorites. He just loves you and wants to be with you. Some friends come and go. Not Jethro. He's always there with a stupid smile on his big furry face. He's inspiring."

Lori thought about these words from the mouth of a 13-year-old, and funny enough, she found that she could tolerate Jethro's shenanigans a little better after that day.

Unfortunately, Ashley was wrong about one thing. Jethro wasn't going to always be there.

When Lori arrived at the vet, she opened the rear hatch of their SUV slowly, reaching one hand underneath the hatch to keep Jethro from jumping out right away. Jethro actually stayed put and waited for Lori to put his collar around his enormous neck and attach the leash.

Lori gave the command and Jethro hopped out of the car onto the walkway.

Jethro actually walked through the vet door without incident this time and began taking in all the smells of the clinic. No other dogs were in the waiting room. Lori checked in and sat on a small bench. Jethro sat right next to her and leaned his massive body weight into her legs. "The Berner Lean." Jethro, the Snuggler.

After just a few minutes the veterinarian emerged with a smile and called Jethro's name. Jethro's ears perked and he stopped panting for a second, tilting his head slightly as if deciding whether to trust this small happy lady wearing scrubs.

The veterinarian approached him gently, but confidently, extending her hand and scratching Jethro behind the ears. Within two seconds she had a friend in Jethro.

The vet asked routine questions as Lori walked Jethro into the examination room. "How is his eating?"

"Fine. He eats as much as a horse."

The vet laughed. "Yes, this breed tends to do that. Has he had any problems or health issues that you've noticed?"

"Nope." Then Lori thought for a moment. "Nothing we've noticed anyway. Although he sure seems like he's been breathing a lot louder lately."

"Hmmm." The vet stroked his neck and chest and then began feeling the area around his collar. All of a sudden her countenance changed. She looked up at Lori.

"What?" Lori asked, seeing that something was noticeably wrong.

The vet didn't answer right away. She checked a few other spots on Jethro's body, then felt his neck again as if she was searching for something.

"How old is Jethro?" The vet finally asked, standing up and looking at his chart.

Lori thought for a minute. "Five. I think."

"Well," the vet replied, "I can't be 100 percent sure, but I think Jethro has lymphoma. We'll need to do a test to be sure."

Lori was numb. She hadn't expected this at all this morning. "What's that mean?" Lori asked.

"It means that he probably only has about 30 to 60 days left with you."

The rest of the visit was spent with the vet telling Lori about chemotherapy options that would cost as much as a car and probably only extend Jethro's life a little bit. They did a quick test and promised to call the next day with the results.

Lori loaded up Jethro in the back of the car. Pulling out onto the main road she let the back window down halfway, just the way Jethro liked it. He poked his gargantuan head out and began enjoying the wind on his face.

Lori was only thinking one thing. *How are we going to tell Ashley?*

The next day the vet called and confirmed her diagnosis. He indeed had lymphoma and wouldn't have much longer, chemo or not.

Ashley took it the hardest, literally bawling when her dad sat her down and told her the news. Jethro had been "her dog" all along; she was the whole reason they got him in the first place. But the whole family was truly brokenhearted about the news.

"I hate knowing! I wish I didn't even know!" Ashley pronounced, tears streaming down her cheeks.

Everyone sat and cried together on the family couch.

It wasn't long before Jethro wandered over, setting his big furry head on Ashley's lap. I guess she was right—he was always there for you. He was the one with cancer, yet he seemed to be the happiest one in the room. Ashley was right. This big furball was actually inspiring.

Life the next week was a little different. Jethro started getting a lot more table scraps. Who cares if they were bad for him! Live it up, Jethro. The family began walking him more, petting him more, hugging him more. They cherished every moment...thankful for the moments they had.

Exactly 36 days later Jethro was gone...but his inspiration lingered on.

TRANSITION STATEMENT

Anyone who has lost a family pet knows the pain that Ashley, Lori, and the family felt. Jethro wasn't just a pet. He was a member of the family and in Ashley's eyes, an inspiration. These times are so hard, and it is especially difficult to find the inspiration and peace to praise the Lord through any kind of loss.

APPLICATION AND SCRIPTURE

Job speaks to us at times like this. He had just experienced a series of major tragedies in his life. He lost way more than a dog; he lost his family, his home, his farm, and all his farm animals. His response is recorded in Job 1:20-21:

20At this, Job got up and tore his robe and shaved his head. Then he fell to the ground in worship 21and said:

"Naked I came from my mother's womb,
and naked I will depart.
The Lord gave and the Lord has taken away;
may the name of the Lord be praised."

It is hard to see how Job could praise God in the giving and taking away. I love the giving part, but the taking away is difficult. Somehow in the midst of tragedy, Job's response is one of worship and praise. Older translations say, "Blessed be the name of the Lord," which is where the popular praise song comes from. In the midst of tragedy Job worships God by offering praise.

Through Job we learn that when God gives we ought to praise God for the inspiration, and when he takes away we ought to praise God for the memory.

Praising God for Giving Inspiration

Praising God when he is giving gifts should be easy, although sometimes even God's gifts can be perceived as a nuisance. Like when Lori mumbled to herself, "Jethro, why do you always have to be right next to us!"

But we can learn a lesson from Ashley when she said, "I like that about Jethro. I find him inspiring!"

The rest of the family didn't see what Ashley saw. They all laughed and said, "What on earth is inspiring about this big doofus?"

But Ashley responded in praise, "He's always happy. Even when life stinks, Jethro is content. There's no drama with Jethro. He doesn't hold grudges, he doesn't play favorites. He just loves you and wants to be with you. Some friends come and go. Not Jethro. He's always there with a stupid smile on his big furry face. He's inspiring."

So many times we don't even see the blessings and inspiration of God. We need to stop and take time in our busy lives to recognize God's gifts like Ashley did.

Praising God for the Memory

When God takes away, we only have a memory. We usually don't sing or dance. We cry. We are sad and wonder, "Why, God?" And that's okay. But let's learn from Job when he said, "Sometimes God takes away, may the name of the Lord be praised."

When people grieve, they often get together and share stories. So often at funerals, people are chosen to share funny stories about the person who has died. Why? It is because those memories are inspiring and healing. They help us cry in laughter and we praise God for the memory of that person. Ashley, Lori, and the other three family members often begin telling stories about the big furball and laugh. Jethro is only a memory now. And that memory is inspiring to them in the sadness they feel.

If you asked Ashley and her family, they wouldn't trade the time they had with Jethro for anything, even though it meant going through pain at the end.

CLOSING

During our short lives God gives us many blessings and takes some away. But in each gift, let's not forget to praise him. And in the gifts that are taken away, let's be like Ashley and remember the inspiration that those gifts gave to us while they were with us. Let's let the memory linger on as a continued inspiration.

Let's pray.

(Suggestion: Look up and print out the lyrics to Matt Redman's "Blessed Be Your Name" and pass them out to your group members as you play the recorded version of the song as a benediction.)

SMALL GROUP QUESTIONS

1. **Around the Circle:** Have you ever had a favorite pet? Tell us about it.

2. **Ask Just a Few:** Have you ever experienced loss? How did you deal with it?

Job is a book in the Bible where we see an individual experience a series of major tragedies in his life. He lost way more than a dog; he lost his family, his home, his farm and all his farm animals. His response is recorded in Job 1:20-21:

[20]*At this, Job got up and tore his robe and shaved his head. Then he fell to the ground in worship* [21]*and said:*

"Naked I came from my mother's womb, and naked I will depart. The Lord gave and the Lord has taken away; may the name of the Lord be praised."

3. **Ask Just a Few:** Why do you think that Job said, "May the name of the Lord be praised"?

4. **Ask Just a Few:** For those who have experienced loss—did you feel like praising God at that time?

5. **Ask Just a Few:** Even though Job was experiencing loss, he recognized that the Lord "gave" him everything to begin with. Did Ashley and her family thank God for what he gave them? What did this look like? (Leader Hint: Ashley's family was able to remember what an inspiration Jethro was, and praise God for his memory.)

6. **Ask Just a Few:** All lives will come to an inevitable end. Should we mourn people's lives just because they'll end someday? (An obvious "no.") Is it wrong to cry when bad things happen? (An obvious "no.") How can we remember to praise God during tough times?

   Say This: As your youth group leader, I'm here for you during those tough times. Feel free to call me when these times come.

TALK 08
TITLE: IGNORING THE SIGNS

TOPICS: Warnings, Pride, Temptation

BIG IDEA: What catches your eye can often cause you to miss the warning signs of danger.

SCRIPTURE

> Samson went down to Timnah and saw there a young Philistine woman. ²When he returned, he said to his father and mother, "I have seen a Philistine woman in Timnah; now get her for me as my wife."
>
> ³His father and mother replied, "Isn't there an acceptable woman among your relatives or among all our people? Must you go to the uncircumcised Philistines to get a wife?" (Judges 14:1-3)

PARTICULARS

This is a true story of a youth group from a church in Modesto, California. Three people ignored the warning signs and died. When I tell this story, I like to show slides of the waterfalls, the trail and the warning sign itself. (If you use Google Images and search for something like "yosemite vernal falls danger waterfall sign," you can usually find a picture of the sign.)

STORY

About 1,500 people per day embark on the "Mist Trail" hike to the top of Vernal Fall in Yosemite National Park each summer. Park Rangers will be the first to tell you that the trails are safe...if you obey the signs.

Three people chose to ignore the signs on a warm July Tuesday in 2011. The record snowfalls that winter resulted in spectacular waterfalls. That meant swifter and more powerful waters, waters that these three individuals would soon underestimate.

Yosemite National Park is truly one of the most beautiful landmarks on the planet, drawing 3 to 4 million visitors per year. Yosemite Valley offers plenty of scenery, hikes and attractions. Some people camp, others stay in gorgeous lodgings like the famous Ahwahnee Hotel. Regardless of where you stay, most people can't help but embark on some of the scenic hikes the valley offers. These hikes range from small hikes, like the 3-mile round trip to Vernal Fall, to all-day hikes, like the 16-mile round trip to Half Dome.

Vernal Fall offers plenty of bang for your buck. In just 1.5 miles you encounter some remarkable scenery. You start at 4,000 feet elevation on a nice wide path. About three quarters of a mile up the trail, you arrive at a bridge with a beautiful view of the falls. Most people can't resist taking countless pictures from this location. Once you resume the hike, the trail quickly turns alongside the river and you begin your ascent. You soon discover why the trail is named "the Mist Trail" as you climb 1,000 feet of 600 stairs carved out of the rock that lead you up and around the picturesque falls. Once up top, you can take a water break and look down at the river below. The spectacular falls drop 317 feet to the rocks below.

Large metal guardrails keep you from slipping into the swift waters. These waters are especially dangerous in the early summer when the snow is mostly melted and the upper lakes are at their fullest.

People typically heed the posted warnings. Large signs are posted near the top, with dogmatic warnings:

Danger: Waterfall!

Stay out of the water! Powerful, hidden currents will carry you over the fall.

Stay back from slippery rock at the water's edge. If you go over the fall, you will die.

That's how the sign actually reads!

A dozen people from a Modesto-area church group embarked on the Vernal Fall hike that beautiful July Tuesday. They arrived at the top about 1:30 in the afternoon, and the sun was hot.

Despite the signs, several members of the group decided to hop the large metal fence and make their way to the edge of the water.

One man brought a young girl near the edge and, despite her screaming, posed for a picture while a teenage girl clicked her camera.

Meanwhile, three in the group actually braved the water 25 feet from the precipice, laughing and enjoying the cool water on their feet.

Several people began shouting at these members of the group, warning them to come back to safety.

The shouts were ignored.

The first to slip on the slick, solid granite river bottom was a 21-year-old girl. It happened so quickly that many didn't even see her slip into the rushing waters. A friend of hers, a male in the group, reached for her, slipping just the same. A third went to reach for them both and was quickly swept into the current as well.

Witnesses looked up as they saw a woman from the group screaming and running along the riverbank. But it was too late. It all happened in a matter of seconds.

Witness Jake Bibee said, "What I will take away with me forever is the look on that grown man's face as he was floating down that river knowing he was going to die and nobody could help them."

Other witnesses say that the first couple grabbed onto each other in desperation as they were swept over the falls, the third went over alone.

Their bodies weren't discovered until months later.

All three were active members of the small Modesto church. All were students. One planned to become a nurse. All three had their lives cut short.

Why?

TRANSITION STATEMENT

A steep trail, rushing water, a huge metal fence, a sign saying *Danger! Stay Out of the Water! You Will Die!* People shouting warnings to come back to safety?

Which of these signs did these three individuals miss?

In the Bible book of Judges is a rather dramatic story of a gifted man of God who ignored the warning signs. The storyteller says that Samson sees a Philistine woman and she "caught his eye."

Samson went down to Timnah and saw there a young Philistine woman. [2]*When he returned, he said to his father and mother, "I have seen a Philistine woman in Timnah; now get her for me as my wife."*

³His father and mother replied, "Isn't there an acceptable woman among your relatives or among all our people? Must you go to the uncircumcised Philistines to get a wife?" (Judges 14:1-3)

That was the pattern of his life. Samson ignored the warning signs because a beautiful woman caught his eye. His parents warned him, "Samson, she is no good for you." But Samson did not listen.

Samson's first warning sign was the advice from his parents who knew the dangers for any person of God to marry a Philistine. They pleaded with him to stay away from her, but Samson was captured by her beauty. He ignored the warning and the consequences were huge. She betrayed him and married the best man at what was supposed to be Samson's wedding. Samson got so livid he spent the next years of his life getting even—revenge. He experienced the emotional pain of rejection, hurt, and uncontrolled anger. His parents were right on.

The climax of the story of Samson was his relationship with another beautiful Philistine woman, Delilah. She kept tying him up, and the idiot couldn't even see what was happening. She was asking him to commit treason—begging him to tell her the way that the Philistines could defeat him and thus all of Israel. It would be as if spies from Al-Qaeda and the Taliban would send sexy women to sleep with our government leaders so that they could find out our secret weapons or battle plans to defeat them. Delilah was a spy.

But Samson treated it like a game. He felt that he could get close to her and not reveal his secret. He reasoned that he could put his toes in the water and not get swept up in the current. Three times Delilah deceived him and finally after her constant nagging he tells her the secret of his strength—his long hair that had never been cut. After she lulled him to sleep in her lap, the Philistines came into her home and shaved his head. He was now so weak that they captured him, poked out his eyes, bound him, and he remained a prisoner until his dramatic death.

As his hair grew, he received back his strength and killed thousands of Philistines, losing his life in the process.

What a tragic story. All the warning signs, but he couldn't see them. What caught his eye blinded him to the warning signs.

CLOSING

Are there warning signs in your life right now?

Are you ignoring them?

Samson was like many of us. We feel that our parents are just so out of touch with our real world. They don't know what it's like to live in our modern world, and they just keep hanging on to old-fashioned ideas. They don't understand. This is where it all starts. But Samson ignored his parents' advice, and he set a pattern of ignoring warning signs.

Today we have many warning signs: Advice from our parents, older and wiser people, the Scriptures, the church, and our friends. But so often we are so captured by something that we either don't see the warning signs or we ignore them. We don't listen to our parents or friends when they advise us, "She is no good for you, son." Or, "That crowd is taking you in the wrong direction." We don't want to hear that advice, so we ignore it.

What are the warning signs that you have been hearing from your parents, your friends, your church, the Scriptures? As we pray, ask God to open your eyes to his warning signs.

Let's pray.

SMALL GROUP QUESTIONS

1. **Around the Circle:** Where is your favorite place to hike, camp, or vacation?

2. **Ask Just a Few:** What were some of the warning signs these three people saw and heard?

3. **Ask Just a Few:** Why do you think they didn't heed the warning?

4. **Around the Circle:** Share about a time when you didn't listen to a warning that you should have.

In the Bible passage we just heard, Samson defied his parents by asking to marry a woman who was really bad news!

Samson went down to Timnah and saw there a young Philistine woman. ²When he returned, he said to his father and mother, "I have seen a Philistine woman in Timnah; now get her for me as my wife."

³His father and mother replied, "Isn't there an acceptable woman among your relatives or among all our people? Must you go to the uncircumcised Philistines to get a wife?" (Judges 14:1-3)

If you read the rest of the story in the book of Judges, you'll discover that this woman tricked Samson and turned him over to his enemies. He never saw any of the warning signs.

5. **Around the Circle:** Why didn't he see the warning signs?

6. **Ask Just a Few:** Why don't we want to see warning signs sometimes?

7. **Around the Circle:** Are there warning signs in your life right now? How are you responding to them?

8. **Around the Circle:** What is one thing we can do this week to open our eyes to warning signs and make efforts to avoid being foolish? How can I, as your leader, help you?

TALK 09
TITLE: A LIFETIME OF DECISIONS

TOPIC: Decision-Making

BIG IDEA: Heroic deeds aren't made in 60 seconds; they are the culmination of a lifetime of wise decisions.

SCRIPTURE

> He was held in greater honor than any of the
> Thirty, but he was not included among the Three.
> And David put him in charge of his bodyguard.
> (1 Chronicles 11:25)

PARTICULARS

Although this is a true story of a national hero, the real story is about his life of little decisions that led up to this huge heroic instant decision that saved 155 lives. It makes a wonderful story and challenge for young people (for all of us).

This story has a lot of small facts to memorize. Some people might want to jot down his "resume" on a notecard for reference.

THE STORY

On January 15, 2009, shortly after takeoff from LaGuardia Airport, Captain Chesley Sullenberger reported to air traffic control that the twin engines of the Airbus A320 he was piloting had shut down after sucking in a flock of birds.

Could he return to LaGuardia? Could he land at the Teterboro Airport in New Jersey? The captain (also known as "Sully") quickly decided that neither option was feasible and determined that ditching in the Hudson River was the only chance for everyone's survival.

Yes. He chose the water.

Sully calmly announced to the passengers to "brace for impact" then piloted the plane to a smooth crash landing in the river about 3:30 p.m.

Sully said, "It was very quiet as we worked, my co-pilot and I. We were a team. But to have zero thrust coming out of those engines was shocking—the silence."

After the plane hit the water, all 155 passengers were evacuated. Sully walked the passenger cabin twice to make sure everyone had left, then he retrieved the plane's maintenance logbook and exited himself.

Every single passenger and crew member survived.

When you only have 30 to 60 seconds to make up your mind about where to land a loaded plane with no engines, what do you do? On one side of the river stood all the high-rise buildings and thousands of people in New York City's Manhattan. On the other side was the heavily traveled New Jersey Turnpike.

How about Newark Airport? It was 12 miles away, and without any engines, you are flying a 170,000-pound glider. You'd never make it 12 miles.

All of this must have been going through Captain Sullenberger's mind in the 60 seconds he had to choose, so he decided to create his own landing strip in the Hudson River. As it turned out, he saved 155 lives that day, and countless others if the plane would have crashed in either city.

The question everyone asked was, *How did he make such a wise, courageous decision under the fire of impending catastrophe?*

Captain Sullenberger summed it up in an interview with Katie Couric: "One way of looking at this might be that for 42 years, I've been making small, regular deposits in this bank of experience: education and training. And on January 15 the balance was sufficient so that I could make a very large withdrawal."

That defining moment wasn't a one-minute decision, but the instinct of a man who had given his life to making wise decisions.

Although New York Governor David Paterson hailed his exploits as the "miracle on the Hudson," those familiar with Sully's background—and his calm under pressure—believed it was less a miracle and more an act that characterized Sully's life as a pilot and safety expert.

Sully instantly became a national hero. President Bush called him and thanked him for saving the lives of passengers. President-elect Obama invited him and his crew to attend his upcoming inauguration ceremony. In addition:

- Sully was honored in his home of Danville, California, where he was given the key to the city and named an honorary Danville police officer.
- New York City Mayor Michael Bloomberg gave Sully the key to a bigger city than Danville.
- Sully threw out the first pitch of the 2009 season for the San

Francisco Giants. The name "Sully" was inscribed on the Giants jersey with the number 155, a reference to the 155 people aboard the plane.

- In 2009 he was awarded the Founders' Medal by The Air League and was ranked second in *Time* magazine's Top 100 Most Influential Heroes and Icons for the year.

- In 2010 he was the Grand Marshal of the Tournament of Roses Parade.

- And of course he was interviewed on major TV news magazine programs such as *60 Minutes.*

What were, in Sully's words, "the deposits of education and training"? When we look at his life and career, we begin to see the bucketloads of "experience deposits" to draw from by the time January 15, 2009, rolled around.

Sully was born in Denison, Texas, to a dentist father and an elementary school teacher mother. According to his only sister, Mary, Sully built model planes and aircraft carriers and became interested in flying after watching jets fly above an Air Force base near his house. He went to school in Denison and was consistently in the 99th percentile in every academic category. At the age of 12, his IQ was high enough join Mensa International. In high school he was the president of the Latin club, first chair flautist, and an honor student.

At 16 Sully learned to fly in an Aeronca 7DC from a private airstrip near his home. He said the training he received from a local flight instructor set his aviation career in motion.

He received his bachelor's degree from the Air Force Academy in 1973, where he majored in psychology and basic sciences and received a plethora of academic awards. He continued his education with two master's degrees—industrial psychology from Purdue University (1973) and public administration from the University of Northern Colorado (1979).

Sully also was an Air Force U.S. F-4 fighter pilot for seven years, attaining the rank of captain and then became a US Airways pilot in 1980.

TRANSITION STATEMENT

Sully was an excellent pilot whom very few people would have ever heard of if it hadn't been for that defining moment when he lost both engines over the Hudson River. In that defining moment he became a hero. But in reality he had built his whole life with the deposits of wise decisions so that in that one moment the proper instincts took over.

APPLICATION AND SCRIPTURE

There is an interesting story in the Bible about a man who was a national hero. If it hadn't been for his defining moments, he would have been a nameless person known as one of the 30. But he faced defining moments, and he was held in "greater honor."

Listen to them.

22Benaiah son of Jehoiada, a valiant fighter from Kabzeel, performed great exploits. He struck down Moab's two mightiest warriors. He also went down into a pit on a snowy day and killed a lion. 23And he struck down an Egyptian who was five cubits tall. Although the Egyptian had a spear like a weaver's rod in his hand, Benaiah went against him with a club. He snatched the spear from the Egyptian's hand and killed him with his own spear. 24Such were the exploits of Benaiah son of Jehoiada; he too was as famous as the three mighty warriors. 25He was held in greater honor than any of the Thirty, but he was not included among the Three. And David put him in charge of his bodyguard. (1 Chronicles 11:22-25)

The storyteller mentions that Benaiah was held in great honor even though he wasn't one of the top three bodyguards. What does that mean? What made him famous?

Benaiah was famous because his instincts kicked in when he met two of Moab's mightiest warriors, and he was able to kill both of them—two against one. He also cornered a lion in a pit on a snowy day (the worst possible foe in the worst possible place under the worst possible conditions) and killed the lion. Then he faced a seven-and-a-half-foot Egyptian warrior, took away the warrior's spear, and killed him with it. Today these exploits would have made the national news. Benaiah probably would have appeared on TV programs. He would have been invited to presidential inaugurations.

Up until that time he was just one of the 30. No name, just one of the 30. In today's sports culture, Benaiah would be like a professional football player who was drafted. He made the team and that is huge. Benaiah was one of the 30 that made the cut. But he was not an all-pro. He was not a Peyton Manning or a Tom Brady.

You see, of all of David's 30 bodyguards, David would name the top three all-pro soldiers. These top three bodyguards were the "special ops" of their day. They were the fiercest of all the soldiers. Benaiah was not one of those three. However, the text tells us that he became more famous than the all-pros—the top three. In fact he was so famous that David put him in charge of the all-pro top three.

Why?

One reason—his exploits. Just like Sully had become famous because of his heroic deed of landing an engineless aircraft in the Hudson, Benaiah also performed some heroic deeds.

To understand the significance of the text, we need to understand that soldiers' training exercises included killing lions. They did this for sport, and it was how they practiced. Even David himself when facing Goliath said that he had killed the lion and bear, and the giant would be just like those beasts to David.

Bodyguards would train and practice so that in the heat of battle they would be able to make quick and smart fighting decisions. That was their job. That is what they did for a living. They didn't practice on simulators or Xbox...they killed real lions.

Benaiah went into the pit and killed it. He didn't fall into a pit and find a lion; he was very intentional about climbing into that pit. Benaiah climbed down into a pit on a snowy day to face the lion. He had so mastered his skill as a warrior, that he was able to make the quick decision to jump into that pit after the lion and say, "Now, I've got you cornered, you won't get away." And that made him famous. This act is so famous that even though it was recorded more than 3,000 years ago, it's still being read in Bible studies and churches today.

CLOSING

So what makes a hero? What made Benaiah so famous? Why did Sully become so famous? It was not just one 60-second decision. It was a lifetime of decisions that led up to the heat of battle. And when they had to make a 60-second decision, their natural instincts took over as they called upon years of practice, experience, calm, skill, education, and courage to act.

Too often it is easy to say when we are young that moral and ethical decisions are not important. We can rationalize that we'll live it up today and make wise decisions tomorrow. But the small, daily decisions define our futures:

- Do I do my homework or skip it and play video games?

- Do I study for this test or party with my friends?

- Do I go along with the group or stand up for what is right?

- Do I resist a temptation or give in to sin?

- No one will ever know, so I can do this stupid thing today.

If we can—like Sully—make small, regular deposits in the bank of ethics, experience, education, training, and morality, then when the real test comes, God will help us make that wise, courageous withdrawal—a heroic decision. At least 155 people are thankful that their pilot had lived a lifetime of wise decisions.

Let's pray.

SMALL GROUP QUESTIONS

1. **Around the Circle:** Share a time when you were in—or almost in—a tragic situation or catastrophe.

2. **Ask Just a Few:** Why was Sully, the pilot, able to make such a smart, quick decision?

3. **Ask Just a Few:** What are some of the "deposits" or wise decisions young people can make today that will prepare them to make a "withdrawal" someday?

4. **Around the Circle:** What are some of the daily decisions that you could change today that might help you become who you want to be tomorrow? How can I, as your youth group leader, help you do that?

TALK 10
TITLE: SURRENDER

TOPIC: Surrendering to God

BIG IDEA: You are a unique creation designed by God for an adventurous journey for good with Christ.

SCRIPTURE

> For we are God's handiwork, created in Christ Jesus to do good works, which God prepared in advance for us to do.
> (Ephesians 2:10)

PARTICULARS

This is a parable I wrote to illustrate complete surrender to live with Christ in life's adventure.

STORY

Trevor, Josh, and Daniel had been stranded on the island for 19 days now. When their small plane went down in the South Pacific, the three men barely escaped, safely parachuting to the beach of the small, uninhabited island.

The first few nights the three castaways were hopeful that someone heard the last-minute distress call sent seconds before jumping from the plane, but when a week passed, that hope slowly faded. The three sunburnt men faced the reality that they might not be just trying to survive a few more nights on coconut milk and sushi. Point of fact, they might need to develop a long-term plan.

The next morning the three men prayed for guidance. As they finished their prayer, each man saw crystal clear what they needed to do.

Unfortunately, they each saw something completely different.

The three men spent most of the day presenting their plans to each other and trying to sell the other two on their idea. But none of them could agree, so finally, the three men agreed to devote their time to their own ideas. They weren't mad at each other. They actually shared tools and resources, but each to their own plan.

Trevor was probably the most pessimistic of the bunch. When he prayed to God, he told him, "How could you let this happen to me? And where are you now? I've been praying day and night for a rescue, and you haven't shown up at all. I guess I'll have to do it on my own."

So Trevor began building himself a boat with oars. He found a fallen tree that had rotted out in the middle and began carving it into a usable shape.

The three men had made some small tools out of rocks and sticks. They fashioned a rock to the end of a branch, tying it with parachute rope to make a hammer. Trevor used another small rock as a chisel. The two tools worked nicely forming his boat. He eventually was able to carve two oars as well and fit them into the notches he made in the side of his boat.

Trevor's first test run proved difficult. As he set the boat in the ocean and tried paddling, the front of the boat was too bulky and didn't cut through the water.

Trevor spent the next few days reshaping the boat, changing the inside so that the front became the back and vice versa. The new front was narrower, and he spent three days sharpening the front of the hull so that it would cut through the water easily.

The next test run was a success. The boat now slid through the water nicely. The oars worked well in the divots he had made in the boat. Each stroke moved the boat with ease.

For the next week, Trevor gathered food and coconuts. He fashioned several long, sharp sticks into spears and organized all these provisions into his boat.

The next morning he said goodbye to his friends, and without a prayer or an acknowledgement to God, he ventured out into the ocean in search of rescue.

Trevor was determined to survive on his own strength!

In the midst of all of this, some of the plane's provisions began washing ashore. Among those provisions was a raft. Neither Trevor nor Daniel was interested in the raft, so Josh gladly used it.

Josh was an interesting fellow. While the other two worked, Josh always seemed to sit around. When the other two would ask, "Aren't you worried about finding some food tonight?" Josh would always reply, "God will provide."

God always did provide. He provided two other guys who would catch fish, pick berries...and then share with Josh.

Before the raft floated ashore, Josh hadn't seemed as eager to build a boat as the other two guys. He thought that building a boat equaled a lack of faith. Josh figured that there was a reason they were all on the island, and he wanted to totally trust in God. But when the raft arrived, Josh saw that as God's provision. Josh agreed with the other two that remaining on the island was futile. But trying to row himself across the Pacific seemed an effort in futility, not to mention a little bit faithless. Josh knew the raft would float him wherever God desired. Josh figured that God knew what was best, and Josh didn't want to get in the way of that.

Josh tested the raft and it floated well. It would be perfect for what Josh wanted—floating wherever God took him.

Josh grabbed the food and provisions that were within arm's reach, prayed, and then set off into the Pacific, floating wherever the ocean took him, confident that God would take care of him.

Josh found faith in God so relaxing. It was so little work, and Josh didn't like work much.

Then there was Daniel.

After several days of praying, Daniel was confident that God hadn't abandoned him. Daniel asked God specifically, "How can I use all that you've given me to survive?"

For some reason, Daniel remembered the story of Moses. He remembered how Moses fled for his life into the desert where he spent 40 years. At the time Moses must have wondered, *Why do I, a man who was raised in an Egyptian palace, have to now live in the desert?* But then God needed someone to step up and lead his people out of Egypt into the desert. God needed a man who knew how to talk to Egyptian rulers and knew how to survive in the desert.

Funny how God works.

Daniel had spent many summers sailing with his father as a boy. He knew sailing. He knew that God could use that knowledge. So Daniel began working on a sailboat.

Daniel's boat project began much like Trevor's. He, too, found a nice log that was hollow in the middle that he began to carve and shape into a boat. But he also designed two horizontal beams that extended out to logs on the side, making the boat look a little like a catamaran. Then he used parachute rope to support the mast, which was secured into a notch in the bottom of the boat and supported by two separate horizontal crossbeams.

Daniel thanked God for providing the parachute. Without the parachute, the whole idea of a "sail" boat probably was pointless. The chute made a perfect sail, also providing plenty of rope, which Daniel would make good use of.

Daniel's first test run was a triumph. The hull of the boat proved strong with no leaks. And his mast held strong. As the wind shifted, he noted a few adjustments he would make to the clew and the boom, but other than that...the vessel was ready.

Daniel spent several days gathering provisions. Like Trevor, Daniel carved several long spears that he could use for spearfishing or to drive away sharks. He also collected so many coconuts that they filled a third of the boat, precluding any chance of Daniel lying flat for sleeping. But Daniel didn't care. He knew that dehydration would be his worst enemy.

Daniel also created a small shade in the corner of the boat out of a little piece of his chute. This would help him avoid too much exposure to the sun. Daniel reflected back to some of the survival training he had received while becoming an Eagle Scout.

After a morning of prayer, Daniel launched his handcrafted sailboat out into the Pacific. The wind came from the south and quickly filled Daniel's sail. The boat picked up speed and cut beautifully through the ocean waters.

As Daniel's boat skipped along, Daniel thanked God.

"God, thanks for providing the food and the coconuts that I have in this boat. Thanks for supplying the log for this boat. Thanks for providing the two friends that helped me make the tools that helped me make this boat. Thanks for the parachute. Thanks for a father who taught me how to sail as a young boy. Thanks for my Eagle Scout training. That knowledge you provided might just save me today."

Daniel turned to the south and felt the wind blow across his face. "And God, now I take all these gifts you've given to me, and I surrender to you...because all these gifts are useless without your wind. So fill my sail with your wind, God. Take me to safety. I surrender all to you!"

Three men left the island within a week's time. One, by his own effort, one, with no effort at all, and one, using the gifts God gave him and surrendering completely to his power.

Three days later the sailboat reached a passing merchant vessel. Within a week Daniel was back home with his wife and kids.

The other two were never seen again.

TRANSITION STATEMENT

The church loves to use the word *surrender*. Pastors will talk about how we need to surrender...I've heard entire sermons preached on "surrendering" to God.

But what does this actually look like?

Does *surrender* mean to just give up and do nothing? Or does it possibly mean something more?

APPLICATION AND SCRIPTURE

God designed each one of us with different talents and abilities that we can use to do good things. The Apostle Paul lays this out for us in Ephesians 2:10:

For we are God's handiwork, created in Christ Jesus to do good works, which God prepared in advance for us to do.

The question is, are we surrendering our talents and abilities to him?

Out of three men stranded on an island, only one really understood what surrender truly means.

It was pretty obvious that the first guy, Trevor, didn't want to surrender. He wasn't an atheist. He knew God was there. Trevor just decided that he wanted to be in charge instead of surrendering to God. If you think about it, Trevor seemed pretty talented and resourceful. Perhaps he just forgot who gave him those talents and who provided those resources. Trevor's downfall wasn't his talents and abilities...it was his pride.

The second guy, Josh, didn't really do anything. He claimed to have faith...but it was an excuse for his own laziness. He wasn't surrendering to God...he was just surrendering to his own slothfulness. Guys like Josh want to have faith like Noah, but they aren't willing to build the boat.

But the third guy, Daniel, got it. He grasped the importance of experiencing God to the fullest. He recognized that he was a unique masterpiece that God had created in his workshop before the creation of the world. God had given Daniel gifts in life that he used to make the journey. Daniel saw how God had gifted him with experiences, skills, and knowledge, so he surrendered those gifts in the hands of God to experience adventure with Christ. Think of the stories he could tell when he got home.

Daniel's prayer demonstrates his relationship with God.

"God, thanks for providing the food and the coconuts that I have in this boat. Thanks for supplying the log for this boat. Thanks for providing the two friends that helped me make the tools that helped me make this boat. Thanks for the parachute. Thanks for a father who taught me how to sail as a young boy. Thanks for my Eagle Scout training. That knowledge you provided might just save me today...And God, now I take all these gifts you've given to me, and I surrender to you...because all these gifts are useless without your wind. So fill my sail with your wind, God. Take me to safety. I surrender all to you!"

How can we experience this kind of relationship with God?

The key to understanding this relationship is through the words, "in Christ Jesus." We were "created in Christ Jesus to do good works." Christ is not just "out there somewhere." Christ is not just some famous teacher who lived a long time ago. He is living in us and we live in him. And this exploration involves doing good works, not just sitting on the beach expecting God to do all the good works. He is with us, and while on that journey we are getting to know him.

CLOSING

Are you looking for purpose and meaning? What could have greater meaning than having a relationship with the Creator of the universe? Before God made all the planets, all the galaxies, the sun, moon, and stars, he designed your unique DNA to do good works with him.

But all the talent and ability in the world are useless without God's power behind it. Are you truly surrendering to God?

Daniel discovered this awesome potential by surrendering his life to God. When I surrender my life to Christ, I pray, "God, how do you want to use me for good?" But I have to say to God, "I'm here. I'm signing up for this adventure. Let's go—you working through me to make it happen. Use my giftedness. I'll do whatever you want me to do."

What knowledge, gifts, and life experiences do you have that God can use for his glory?

Let's pray.

SMALL GROUP QUESTIONS

1. **Around the Circle:** Share a time when you were lost as a kid.

2. **Ask Just a Few:** What mistake did the first guy, Trevor, make? Explain.

3. **Ask Just a Few:** What about the second guy, Josh? What was his problem? Explain.

4. **Ask Just a Few:** What did Daniel do that the other two didn't?

God designed each one of us with different talents and abilities that we can use to do good things. The Apostle Paul lays this out for us in Ephesians 2:10:

For we are God's handiwork, created in Christ Jesus to do good works, which God prepared in advance for us to do.

5. **Ask Just a Few:** What does Paul describe us as? What does "God's handiwork" mean?

6. **Ask Just a Few:** What were we created for? What might this look like?

7. **Ask Just a Few:** What are some of the gifts and abilities God gives to his "handiwork"?

8. **Around the Circle:** What are some of your gifts?

9. **Around the Circle:** How can you surrender those gifts to God so he can do good works through you? How can I, as your youth group leader, help you do that?

TALK 11
TITLE: A SECOND CHANCE

TOPICS: Social Justice, Missions, Fresh Start

BIG IDEA: God inherently values those whom the world labels worthless.

SCRIPTURE

> [35]For I was hungry and you gave me something to eat, I was thirsty and you gave me something to drink, I was a stranger and you invited me in, [36]I needed clothes and you clothed me, I was sick and you looked after me, I was in prison and you came to visit me.
>
> [37]"Then the righteous will answer him, 'Lord, when did we see you hungry and feed you, or thirsty and give you something to drink? [38]When did we see you a stranger and invite you in, or needing clothes and clothe you? [39]When did we see you sick or in prison and go to visit you?'
>
> [40]"The King will reply, 'Truly I tell you, whatever you did for one of the least of these brothers and sisters of mine, you did for me.'" (Matthew 25:35-40)

PARTICULARS

The following story about Shoaf and Father G are true stories about ministry to felons. We often talk about the words of Jesus and how he hung out with the disenfranchised of society, but we don't know how to do it. This is an exciting story of how one person followed Christ's example. I would use this story in two ways. First to talk about God's love and redemption to those who feel huge guilt because of past sin and have a hard time accepting God's forgiveness. But second, to challenge the youth group to reach out to those whom society rejects—people like those who have to check "felon" on their applications for work.

Even though this talk really has a spiritual growth focus, it also provides a great opportunity to give an invitation to those who'd like a "second chance" and want to experience God's love and grace. I kept the spiritual growth focus of the talk, inspiring young people who are already believers to show Jesus' love to the outcasts of society, but you may want to consider also giving an invitation. We never know who is sitting in our audience. And even if we are talking to 99 people about how they can grow in their faith, we might want to extend an invitation to the one person who hasn't put their trust in Jesus yet. I believe we can give these kinds of invitations without watering down our messages. This talk is a perfect example. Feel free to adjust the wrap-up to the venue that works for your audience.

STORY

This is the story of two men in the streets of L.A. and where their lives intersected. One man was a felon. The other was a priest.

Shoaf never wanted to get in trouble. His friends would attest that Shoaf is usually calm, considerate, and charming, but when pushed he can be explosive. He grew up on the streets of Los Angeles in a Crip area and was arrested for an assault when he was 18. For the next 10 years Shoaf spent his time in and out of prison.

Prison is incredibly tough. But life after prison can prove tougher.

One of the biggest challenges that Shoaf faced after prison was finding a job. He would spend all day filling out applications and trying to get hired; but he had a huge obstacle—he was a felon. When it came time to check the box where he had to say he had committed a felony, he was honest. After turning in his applications for work, he would wait and wait, but no one called. Finally he lied on an application to work in the deli at Ralph's and did not check the felony box. Leaving it blank, he was hired.

He avoided the conversation with his parole officer as long as he could and would even skip parole meetings to keep from having to tell his PO that he had lied on the application. When his PO directly asked Shoaf if his boss knew he was a felon, he admitted the truth.

To Shoaf's surprise, when he told his supervisor, she was fine with Shoaf's past because she said that he was one of her best workers. In fact, she was going to put him on the register—a huge promotion for him. However, Shoaf's PO wasn't comfortable with the lie and made sure that Shoaf got fired.

Shoaf was embarrassed, angry, and lost. He left the halfway house where he was staying and slept in his car until his PO sent him back to jail on what he called a technical violation. This time when he got out of jail, he had no prospects for work. He lived with his girlfriend for a while, but when they broke up, he was back on the street. He spent a few nights with a friend, but when his friend got in a fight with his girlfriend and it got rough, Shoaf intervened. Shoaf panicked as he felt himself losing control once again. Afraid that he'd be sent back to prison again, he left his friend's apartment and slept in his car each night parked behind a Burger King. Each morning he would go to his friend's apartment to iron a shirt so he could go out and apply for work.

In January 2010 Shoaf wandered into a job interview with little confidence. It was there that Shoaf's life intersected with the other key player in this story, Father Gregory Boyle, known as Father G in the neighborhood. Father G had a ministry that gave jobs to felons called Homeboy Industries. Father G not only gave Shoaf a job...he gave him hope.

Homeboy Industries was the vision and passion of Father G and has totally restored the lives of hundreds of ex-cons.

When Father G arrived in Boyle Heights in the 1980s, he began preaching at the Dolores Mission, which was a tiny yellow church with a Spanish-tile roof. Every night Father G took a walk through the rough neighborhood. Gang members would watch him walk, wondering what he was doing, and the police would stop him, thinking that he was there for drugs.

Father G began making an impact when he would visit victims of a shooting or a fight in the hospital. He had a great knack for picking up the street slang and began to incorporate it into his own vocabulary. Most of the gang members were Latino, and Father G said that when they were running from the police, they would cross themselves as they ran by his church.

Father G wasn't afraid to step into the middle of a fight. A defining moment came when 50 or 60 gang members were going at it with baseball bats and blocking four lanes of traffic. Father G ran into the middle of the gangs and yelled, "Put down the mother***king bats!"

"It was like the parting of the Red Sea," Father G remembers. The crowd quieted, and then one of them spoke, "Father G...you cursed!"

Since some of the neighbors saw how Father G's walks were having a calming effect on the neighborhood, they bought him a bike so that he could cover more ground. As he rode his bike through the neighborhood, he became aware of what he called the number one problem facing the community—the lack of jobs. When young men and women couldn't find work, they had no hope. This was especially true for the young men who had spent time in prison.

So Father G began a whole new ministry—finding jobs for men. When he couldn't find jobs, he started creating jobs. In 1992 he got a large donation from a movie producer, and he took over a small bakery. This was the beginning of Homeboy Industries.

One of the most unusual businesses that Father G started was tattoo removal. He had never planned to add that kind of service to Homeboy Industries, but trying to find work for a young man who had tattooed on his forehead, F*** the World, he knew he had to find a doctor who would remove the tat. Next thing Father G knew he was in the tattoo removal business.

Father G has an unusual business plan. He does not start a business because he has a passion for a particular business. He starts a business to create jobs. That is his mission. He says, "We don't hire homies to bake bread, we bake bread to hire homies. If you are in downtown L.A. and want a taco, you know to go to Homeboy's and be served by homegirls who are just out of prison. That's what makes Homeboy so unique. It is a ministry, a business, and a living example of second chances."

Homeboy employs hundreds of ex-cons, whom Father G calls his homies, and it is one of the country's largest gang-intervention programs. In addition to jobs, he offers free tattoo removal, GED classes, and counseling to thousands.

Because of his best-selling book, *Tattoos on the Heart: The Power of Boundless Compassion*, he has become quite famous. He's even a tourist attraction. People from all over the country will stop by to get a picture and have him autograph their copy of his book. But all of this has not gone to his head. He just likes to be called Father G, and he calls all his employees by affectionate nicknames such as *son, kiddo, dawg,* and *mijo*.

As a priest he marries them, baptizes their children and, at times, he has to bury them.

Father G is really just delivering what his heavenly Father abounds in...second chances. That's what he offered to a felon named Shoaf.

When Shoaf found himself in jail one last time, Father G visited him and told Shoaf, "The day you get out of prison, you have your job back." Shoaf not only had a job, he became a supervisor. All because a man nicknamed Father G was willing to give him a second chance.

TRANSITION STATEMENT

Wouldn't it be nice to be given a second chance?

Sure, maybe you're not a felon...but when you mess up, however you mess up, wouldn't it be nice to have someone who says, "I don't care about your past, let's look at your future!"

That's what Father G offers to felons. And that's what Jesus offers to you! As a matter of fact, Jesus is so adamant about love and forgiveness, that he warns his believers what will happen to them if they aren't willing to extend grace.

APPLICATION AND SCRIPTURE

Preachers love to talk about how Jesus spent his time with prostitutes, thieves, murderers, and the outcasts of society. But are these just words? How many of us really show love to people whom society rejects?

Failing to follow Christ's example has some huge consequences.

At the close of Jesus' ministry he tells an interesting story. In this

Source: "House of Second Chances," Douglass McGray, *Fast Company*, April 16, 2012

story Jesus describes the final judgment scene at the end of time. The King divides the people into two groups—the sheep and the goats. He invites all of the sheep to live with him in his eternal kingdom. But he does not invite the goats to live in his kingdom. He rejects them.

So an important question of the parable is, "who are the sheep and who are the goats?" Or another way to ask this question is, "who gets to live with the King in his eternal kingdom?" Jesus answers that question in the conclusion of the story in Matthew 25:35-40:

35For I was hungry and you gave me something to eat, I was thirsty and you gave me something to drink, I was a stranger and you invited me in, 36I needed clothes and you clothed me, I was sick and you looked after me, I was in prison and you came to visit me.

37"Then the righteous will answer him, 'Lord, when did we see you hungry and feed you, or thirsty and give you something to drink? 38When did we see you a stranger and invite you in, or needing clothes and clothe you? 39When did we see you sick or in prison and go to visit you?'

40"The King will reply, 'Truly I tell you, whatever you did for one of the least of these brothers and sisters of mine, you did for me.'

In this prophetic parable, Jesus says the difference between the sheep and the goats is how they treat him (just like when he was on earth). Who accepted Christ on earth? Sinners. Who rejected Christ on earth? The so-called "righteous, religious" community. Jesus predicts that many in the church will do the same. Jesus says he was hungry, thirsty, homeless, in prison, and sick. The so-called "righteous" are shocked and ask the King, "When did we ever see you hungry, thirsty, sick, and in prison?" In Jesus' answer to their question he uses the telling phrase, "the least of these" to refer to the outcast, the oppressed, the poor, the sick, and the prisoners. They are not the "least" as far as God is concerned.

CLOSING

God inherently values those whom the world labels worthless.

But no one is worthless in God's sight. Every homie, prisoner, gang member, and thief is worth the life of God's only Son, Jesus.

There are huge consequences for not recognizing the worth of all people. God doesn't hold back his judgment on the importance of valuing all people.

So often the church quotes the words of Jesus about how the sick need a physician, but church leaders, including youth groups, are afraid or don't know how to minister to the bitter and disenfranchised people. We have a huge responsibility as Christians, and even as a youth group, to try and help those kids who are the rejected kids, those who have been in gangs, have been in juvie, and those who are in huge need.

How can we do that?

A way to begin is to be like Jesus and Father G, and not just hang out with the cool kids, but reach out to the kids who are not like us. What does this look like for you this week?

Think of someone you know who is rejected by everyone. Maybe it even seems like they deserve it. But what if you did the unthinkable and reached out and gave them a second chance?

Someday, God will look at you face to face and say, "Thanks. Because whatever you did for one of the least of these brothers and sisters of mine, you did for me."

Let's pray.

OPTIONAL INVITATION

If you're sitting here tonight and thinking, *I'm tired of living life selfishly. I really need a second chance,* Jesus is offering you a second chance right now. He doesn't care where you've been, but he cares where you are going.

If you'd like a fresh start, Jesus can wipe your slate clean and give you a fresh start. That new life begins with putting your trust in him and telling him, "Please forgive me for my past, I give you my future." Putting trust in Christ isn't easy. Because trusting him means putting aside the way we lived our past, and letting him control our future. Does this mean we have to be perfect? No, it just means that we need to be willing to let him slowly make us perfect. That's where trust comes in.

If you want to pray that prayer, we can pray that prayer with you right now.

SMALL GROUP QUESTIONS

1. **Around the Circle:** Who is the most caring and loving person you have ever met? Describe that person.

2. **Ask Just a Few:** How did Father G give convicts like Shoaf hope?

Jesus describes how we should treat those in need in the conclusion of his story in Matthew 25:35-40:

[35]For I was hungry and you gave me something to eat, I was thirsty and you gave me something to drink, I was a stranger and you invited me in, [36]I needed clothes and you clothed me, I was sick and you looked after me, I was in prison and you came to visit me.

37"Then the righteous will answer him, 'Lord, when did we see you hungry and feed you, or thirsty and give you something to drink? 38When did we see you a stranger and invite you in, or needing clothes and clothe you? 39When did we see you sick or in prison and go to visit you?'

40"The King will reply, 'Truly I tell you, whatever you did for one of the least of these brothers and sisters of mine, you did for me.'

God inherently values those whom the world labels worthless.

3. **Ask Just a Few:** What were some of the ways that the righteous people helped the needy in this parable?

4. **Ask Just a Few:** When the righteous people were helping the needy, who were they actually helping...according to Jesus? (v. 40) Why is this?

5. **Ask Just a Few:** Who are some of the people that the world treats as worthless?

6. **Ask Just a Few:** How can we help people feel as though they have worth and hope?

7. **Around the Circle:** What is something you can do this week to reach out to someone whom the world labels "worthless"? How can I, as your youth group leader, help you do that?

TALK 12
TITLE: SOCKS

TOPICS: Faith, Trust, Suffering

BIG IDEA: It's hard to consider it joy during difficult times because we don't know the whole story.

SCRIPTURE

James is writing to Christians who are under great persecution, and he is instructing them to "consider it joy" when they are facing hard times.

> [2]Consider it pure joy, my brothers and sisters, whenever you face trials of many kinds, [3]because you know that the testing of your faith produces perseverance. [4]Let perseverance finish its work so that you may be mature and complete, not lacking anything.
> (James 1:2-4)

PARTICULARS

This is a true story about my family. It was a lesson to each of us about how we often fail to see the best God has for us when we are facing tough times. You can use our story, or perhaps you have had a similar experience with your family that you can use instead to introduce the James passage.

STORY

Ashley didn't like cats much...until she met Socks.

Socks wasn't like most cats Ashley had encountered. He wasn't shy, distant, or moody. In fact, Socks was a cuddler.

Ashley first met Socks when she was on the back patio painting her toenails. She heard a noise and looked up to find Socks perched on the fence watching Ashley at work. He was gray with a white chest and feet.

Ashley greeted him. "Hi, there."

Socks tilted his head slightly, then yawned.

Ashley chuckled at the cat's "chill" attitude and resumed painting her big toe.

A few moments later the confident gray kitty jumped down from the fence and assuredly walked on the patio for a closer look. Ashley noticed a prominent scar on his left ear and a few scratches around his body. No collar, not fixed, a little thin...this cat with the little white paws was most likely a stray.

"I'll call you Socks," Ashley pronounced. What else would you call this cat with the little white paws?

Socks sniffed the bottle of toenail polish and then Ashley's wet toenails. He paused, and sneezed, shaking his head. Ashley laughed. "I know. It stinks. Don't get high on this stuff!"

Socks circled Ashley, finally plopping down next to her left leg. Ashley paused her artwork and gave Socks a scratch behind the ears.

"Hey buddy."

She began petting the cat's smooth gray coat. His fur was short and soft.

"Do you have a home?"

Socks looked up at Ashley for a moment and then laid his head down. Ashley felt his purring against her leg. The two sat together on the patio, enjoying the cool breeze and listening to the birds singing in the nearby birch. This was the first moment of many for them.

Ashley didn't see Socks for a week. She almost forgot about him until one moment during breakfast she saw him lounging in the backyard. Ashley walked outside, chewing on her toast. Socks watched her but didn't move from his resting spot. Ashley sat down on that familiar spot on the patio, taking another bite of her jelly-coated toast. Eventually Socks stood and stretched, yawning.

Ashley snickered, "I hear ya. It's too early! At least you don't have to go to school!"

Socks wandered over and immediately began sniffing Ashley's toast. She held it out so he could get a better peek. Without hesitation, he began licking jelly off the top.

Ashley laughed. "Sure, go ahead. I was done anyway."

But as he licked, Ashley couldn't help but notice how skinny the stray was. She left the remainder of the toast on the ground and went inside to get some milk. Isn't that what you're supposed to give cats?

A moment later Ashley returned with a bowl of milk, and Socks gladly lapped it up. Ashley went inside and began scanning through the pantry.

Tuna!

As she was opening up the can of tuna, Ashley's brother and sister came down for breakfast.

"Tuna?" her sister muttered. "I thought you didn't like tuna!"

"I don't," Ashley replied candidly, not offering anything else.

Ashley finished opening the can and walked outside. Her brother and sister looked at each other, confused, then followed.

Socks seemed to smell the can of tuna before the door was even open. He abandoned the bowl of milk and began meowing as soon as Ashley opened the door. Ashley set down the tuna and Socks dug in.

Ashley's brother and sister began asking Ashley endless questions. She fielded the questions with confidence.

"Where did he come from?"

"I don't know. Just showed up."

"How long has he been here?"

"Since last week."

"Is this one of our neighbor's cats?"

"Don't think so. No collar. I think he's a stray."

Ashley's brother began petting Socks as the cat continued ingesting the tuna in sheer delight.

"He's got a lot of scars."

"Yeah," Ashley replied. "He's been in a lot of fights."

The tuna must have been a raging success because the next morning Socks was on the back patio again. He returned day after day for milk and tuna, eventually earning favor with the entire house.

"I think it's time to buy some cat food," Ashley's mom finally proposed. "The tuna is running dry."

The seasons passed and the family's love for Socks grew. Ashley's brother made a little carpeted kitty palace, and her dad bought two kitty bowls which Ashley kept filled with water and food.

It wasn't uncommon to see Ashley or her siblings lying on the back patio with Socks snuggled up next to them, getting his head scratched, closing his eyes and purring in bliss.

But one day Socks didn't show up.

Three days passed.

"Have you seen Socks?" Ashley asked her brother and sister.

"I don't know. I don't think so."

Ashley was worried.

A few more days passed. No Socks.

"Dad, Socks hasn't been at our house for six days."

"Don't worry, Baby," her dad offered. "Socks probably found some cute little tabby somewhere. He'll be back."

Ashley wasn't satisfied.

Three more days passed. Ashley was eating breakfast when she saw him. He was at the back door staring inside. But something was wrong with his ear.

Ashley raced to the door. Socks greeted Ashley with a meow. His left ear had a chunk missing and was scabbed over. As she bent down to pet him she noticed it wasn't just his ear that was hurt. He had a huge gash down his left side. Socks winced when Ashley's fingers got near the gash, but he didn't stop cuddling next to her.

Ashley went inside. "Dad, you have to look at Socks. He's hurt!"

Within a minute the whole family was on the back patio inspecting Socks and speculating about what had happened.

"He got in a fight," Ashley's brother declared.

"It looks like he lost," her mom replied.

Ashley wasn't listening. She was just worried about the cat. So was her dad, who was inspecting the dried blood on Sock's ear.

"I don't think we can do anything about this right now," her dad finally offered. "I think time will heal this."

Ashley objected, but it didn't do any good. Her dad insisted that they give it some time.

Socks appeared again the next morning. The gash on his side didn't look any better. If anything, it looked worse. The following day, Sock's wounds definitely looked worse. When Ashley's dad got home that night, she immediately brought him to the back patio.

"It's worse, Dad!"

Her dad didn't argue. "We need to get him to the vet."

"But what if he hates the car?"

Ashley thought of her Uncle Thom's cat. "Remember how Goliath hates the car!"

"I know. That's why Thom uses that cat carrier. We need to get one of those."

An hour later the family gathered around Socks on the back patio.

Ashley held Socks, while her dad placed a cat carrier on the patio table, quietly opening the door.

"I don't think he's going to like this," Ashley said.

She slowly started lifting him toward the carrier.

Socks sensed what was going on. He buckled, quickly jumped from Ashley's arms and fled, easily climbing the back fence and disappearing. His back claws scratched Ashley's arms as he leapt. Ashley rubbed the cuts as everyone stood there trying to take in what had just happened.

"He didn't mean it," Ashley said, her hand covering the scratches. "He was just trying to jump down."

She was right. The frightened cat didn't mean to hurt Ashley. He was just trying to avoid the crate.

"He's scared," Ashley's dad explained. "He doesn't know that we're trying to help him. We'll have to try again next time we see him."

The next morning Socks returned. Ashley's dad brought out a can of tuna and set it on the ground. Ashley heard the back door open and rushed down from her room to see, joining her dad and Socks on the back patio.

Ashley's dad looked at her and put his finger to his lips.

Socks ate the tuna quietly. Ashley's dad petted him softly and eventually picked him up. Socks complied. Socks had always been gentle with the family.

Ashley's dad turned toward the open door of the crate and slowly began to place Socks inside. When Socks was about a foot from the door, his body flinched once again. But this time Ashley's dad held tight. Socks scratched with his back claws, immediately drawing blood on Ashley's dad's arms. The struggle was only a few seconds, and eventually Socks had lost this battle. But Ashley's dad wasn't without battle wounds.

As Ashley's dad latched the door, Ashley started crying.

"Daddy, you're hurt!"

Her dad went inside, wet a paper towel, and began dabbing at the scratches all over his arms. Eventually he grabbed his keys.

"We need to get him to the vet."

On the way to the vet Ashley asked. "Dad, why did Socks scratch us? Didn't he know we were trying to help him?"

"I guess not, Baby. We know the whole story. We know that we're actually helping Socks, but Socks can't see that. Socks just sees the situation as a threat. He thinks we're shoving him in this small crate, and he doesn't understand why."

TRANSITION STATEMENT

The comment by Ashley's father makes me wonder if the Holy Trinity ever discusses the trials that we are going through. I imagine at times that as they observe the pain we experience on earth, the Father says to the Son, "They don't think that we are actually helping them. They only see the situation as a threat. They think that we are just shoving them in a crate—they don't see the whole story."

APPLICATION AND SCRIPTURE

James is writing to Christians who are under great persecution, instructing them to "consider it pure joy" when facing hard times.

²Consider it pure joy, my brothers and sisters, whenever you face trials of many kinds, ³because you know that the testing of your faith produces perseverance. ⁴Let perseverance finish its work so that you may be mature and complete, not lacking anything. (James 1:2-4)

Yeah, right. Consider it joy when you suffer. Sure. Easy to say.

That is what James is saying. But what is so great about James' command is that he is not just telling them to think positively. He tells them why. He gives to them a reason to count it joy when they are pushed into a cage. He is giving them a reason that they can count it joy to experience the pain and suffering. Look at the reasons why we can count it joy—we are part of a process of developing strength.

Think of sports and grades. Without struggle, you are just average. To improve your personal best time on the mile, or improve your batting average, or increase your SAT score, it takes the pain of delayed gratification—scheduling the pain of the study, workouts, and tons of practice so that you can enjoy the pleasure of improvement. And if you can't see the goal, you can't see the joy of perseverance. James says that this is the way to maturity and completeness so that you lack nothing.

But like Socks the cat, we live in the now and do what we think is best. So we fight God.

But James doesn't stop there, because he knows that it is hard to count it joy when we don't understand the process of a goal of the Christian—to be complete and lacking nothing. James says that if we ask God for wisdom during this process, God will give it to us—when we have the faith to believe him.

⁵If any of you lacks wisdom, you should ask God, who gives generously to all without finding fault, and it will be given to you. ⁶But when you ask, you must believe and not doubt, because the one who doubts is like a wave of the sea, blown and tossed by the wind. ⁷That person should not expect to receive anything from the Lord. [8]Such a person is double-minded and unstable in all they do.

Sock's basic problem was that in that moment he just didn't trust that Ashley and her family wanted the best for him. Socks was suspicious of their actions. He was willing to eat their food and drink their milk and soak in their love, but that is all he wanted. He could have had so much more if he truly believed that they had his best in mind. Unfortunately Socks is just a cat and doesn't have that ability to reason.

So what's our excuse?

CLOSING

How about you? Are you fighting God right now because you want your way? Are you struggling with trust and faith in God who really loves you and wants the best for you? Let's pray for the wisdom that God promises to all who ask so that we can believe in an end result of joy.

Let's pray.

SMALL GROUP QUESTIONS

1. **Around the Circle:** Which do you like better, dogs or cats? Why?

2. **Ask Just a Few:** Why did the cat resist going in the little cat carrier?

3. **Ask Just a Few:** What was Ashley's dad trying to do?

4. **Ask Just a Few:** Describe how God might be trying to help people, but they don't see the whole story.

James wrote to Christians who were under great persecution and instructed them to "consider it pure joy" when they faced hard times.

²Consider it pure joy, my brothers and sisters, whenever you face trials of many kinds, ³because you know that the testing of your faith produces perseverance. ⁴Let perseverance finish its work so that you may be mature and complete, not lacking anything. (James 1:2-4)

5. **Ask Just a Few:** What did James tell us to do when we face trials?

6. **Ask Just a Few:** James tells us to consider it pure joy when we face trials because we know...something. What do we know?

7. **Ask Just a Few:** God has our best in mind when we endure trials. He knows they make us stronger and able to endure. How does "knowing this" help us persevere through tough times?

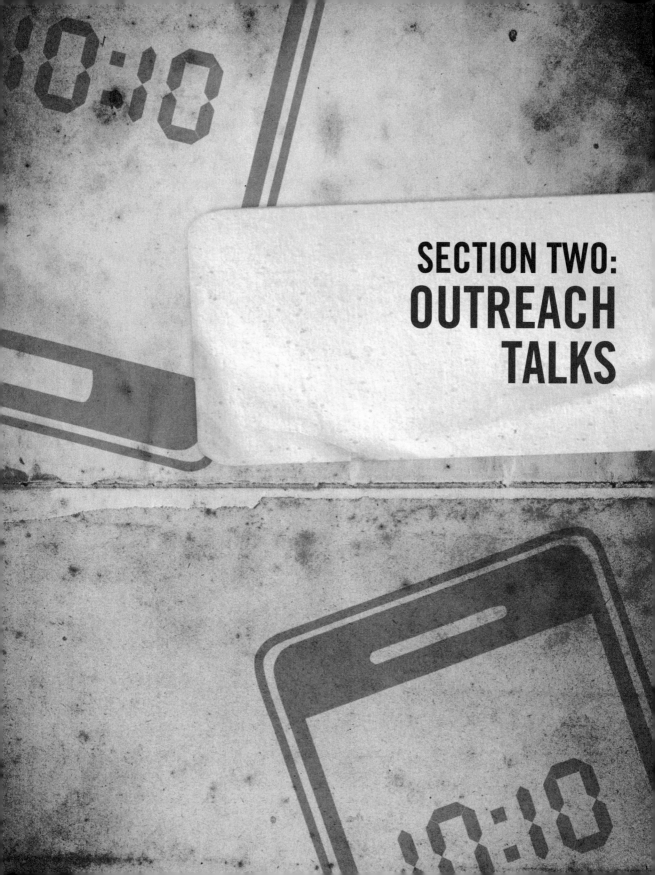

SECTION TWO:
OUTREACH TALKS

TALK 13
TITLE: THE TRAPS OF SUCCESS

TOPICS: Success, Seeking Satisfaction

BIG IDEA: Even though we have it all, the life of excess will never satisfy.

SCRIPTURE

> All things are wearisome,
> more than one can say.
> The eye never has enough of seeing,
> nor the ear its fill of hearing. (Ecclesiastes 1:8)

PARTICULARS

This is a 21st-century telling of the story of Solomon. Solomon was a gifted leader and a huge success; but he had one problem—excess. He tried to fill his empty life with more—more money, power, and sex. Many of us have witnessed this story in the lives of real people—celebrities, athletes, and successful business leaders. The story is repeated in the Bible through many characters. We need to be reminded over and over again, because the temptation to live a life of excess is so alluring, and we all think that we can handle it. Very few have. So I'll tell the story again.

STORY

Justin was born driven. When he was six years old he had a lemonade stand that funded his first Gameboy system within a month's time. By age 12 he was mowing the lawns of 10 different homes in his neighborhood and snow blowing driveways in the winter.

Justin wasn't gifted with initiative and a keen business sense only; he also had natural ability academically and athletically. His freshman year of high school he made the varsity football team as a wide receiver. And sports never interfered with his grades. He was at the top of his class.

Justin also had a knack for technology. Maybe it was all those early years spent with Mario and Luigi, or perhaps it was the fact he had networked every computer and game system in his house by age 11 so he and his brothers could play multiplayer from their own rooms. If there wasn't an existing solution to a problem, Justin usually invented one. That's probably why Justin had a paid internship at MacTel his sophomore year. MacTel had never processed employee paperwork for someone who didn't even have a driver's license.

But football, school, gaming, and work hadn't interfered with Justin's dedication to God and church. Justin was raised at Christ Community Church not three miles from his house. He loved God and he surrounded himself with good friends. By his junior year he was the student leader in charge of the entire Mexico mission trip, leading more than 100 students, and pretty much leading the 20-plus adults as well. This time in Mexico was special to him. For some reason, in the midst of all this dirt and poverty...he experienced a joy like no other, a joy that came from simply using his gifts as a leader to serve God.

Justin was a born leader.

Universities began the bidding war over Justin as soon as he set his eyes on the college horizon. Michigan State and Notre Dame wanted him for football, Dartmouth wanted him for his academics, and Berkeley wanted him for the environmental initiative he had designed for MacTel. Justin actually helped MacTel set up a 501(c)3 nonprofit organization, which worked on preserving the Atlantic shoreline. Within a year more than 60 percent of MacTel employees allocated a percentage of their paychecks to help the cause.

It was right around this time that Justin began seeing Lindsey.

Lindsey and Justin went out for the first time their junior year when she was homecoming queen and he was homecoming king. Justin knew Lindsey from football—Lindsey was a cheerleader. She wasn't in any of his honor classes, but Justin didn't care. She was the most beautiful creature he had ever seen.

By Justin's senior year, his relationship with Lindsey was pretty serious. He told himself not to get involved, because he knew he would be going away to college. But Lindsey captivated him. Every time he was with her he couldn't control himself. That's why they started having sex regularly. Justin told himself, "I'm in love. She's the one. There's no way this could be wrong when it feels this right."

Justin bought Lindsey everything she wanted. He made more money than any teenager in his school, and he wasn't saving a dime for college because he knew he had a full ride anywhere he wanted. So Justin began splurging on every cool little gadget that technology offered, and every piece of clothing that Lindsey desired.

Justin began to drift away from church his senior year. With football, Lindsey, MacTel...Lindsey...and Lindsey...Justin didn't even go on the Mexico mission trip that year. It was the first time he missed it. Instead he spent spring break with Lindsey at Daytona Beach. MacTel actually had a conference down there, so that was his excuse, as far as his parents knew. Justin spent the week on the beach and in a hotel with Lindsey living the good life.

What more could a 17-year-old want? He had money, sex, stuff...is there anything more?

Lindsey cried for a week when Justin made his decision to move to the West Coast and go to Stanford. Lindsey was community college-bound and destined to stay in their small East Coast town for life.

But Justin didn't forget about Lindsey.

By the end of his freshman year Justin was offered a position at Mac-Tel's West Coast headquarters in Seattle. They didn't even want him to finish at Stanford. This kid was the LeBron James of technology. They gave him an offer he couldn't refuse.

Justin accepted the job, immediately leased an apartment in the Seattle downtown with a view of the Space Needle, and flew Lindsey out, greeting her at the airport with a five-carat flawless diamond in an elegant white gold setting.

The two were married. Within three years Justin was CEO of MacTel.

At 22 Justin was on the cover of *Forbes*, *Fast Company*, and even hosted *Saturday Night Live*. Justin became a household name. That didn't hurt his pursuits at starting his own company as soon as his "non-compete" clause ended with MacTel. His company was called e-Vi.

e-Vi went public in a year, and the stock immediately skyrocketed. With Justin's ingenuity at the helm, e-Vi was taking technology to places that MacTel had only dreamed about.

As Justin expanded e-Vi's influence, his position required travel, both nationally and internationally. It was on one of these early business trips that Justin met Mackenzie. Mackenzie worked in the bar at the Hyatt in downtown Manhattan. Justin tipped her a $100 bill, and she left her phone number.

Justin's night with Mackenzie in the penthouse suite of the Hyatt was just the first of many. Justin hooked up with Mackenzie every time he found himself in Manhattan, or even in New Jersey.

But Justin tried to maintain his straight-laced reputation. He gave $10 million to a local church in Seattle for their new building. A year later Justin spent $20 million on his own home in a beautiful, coastal Seattle suburb. Granted he spent fewer than 100 nights a year at home— the rest of the time he traveled or spent stretches at his Maui home or his Florida home. That wasn't including the apartment he secretly bought for Mackenzie.

Justin's philandering expanded beyond Mackenzie. He had Taylor in Miami, and Stephanie, the stripper he met in Chicago. Strip clubs had become a regular stop for Justin in his travels. He found that alcohol and women were great icing on the cake for many of his business deals. It wasn't rare to find Justin courting other executives with call girls and limitless bar tabs.

Lindsey eventually found out about the women, but after weighing the alternatives, she decided to ignore Justin's philandering. She turned to prescription meds for comfort. As her addiction grew worse, Justin simply paid doctors to give her heavier meds.

Justin and Lindsey had two boys. Neither parent set any limits, so they grew up spoiled and chemically dependent like their mother.

When Justin turned 50, he grew tired of the fast pace and weary of the partying. Nothing seemed to fill the void in his life anymore. He had anything and everything he wanted...yet he was miserable.

He passed on e-Vi to his kids and retired with Lindsey to the house in Maui. Within five years the company split under the mismanagement of Justin's sons, and the stocks plummeted.

The day his company split, Justin wept. It was a glaring metaphor of what his life had become.

He cried out to God in guilt and regret. He looked back nostalgically at one of the happiest moments in his life, in the dirt of Mexico, praising God, helping the needy, and telling others the truth about Jesus.

Justin looked over everything he had created. He looked at his houses, his investment portfolio, his family...everything...and he said one word.

"Meaningless."

TRANSITION STATEMENT

Justin is the 21st-century picture of one of the greatest leaders in the Bible—Solomon. He was oozing with talent, street smarts, and leadership ability. But he was driven to excess. Nothing could fulfill his need for more.

APPLICATION AND SCRIPTURE

As Solomon looked back on his empty life, he wrote the book of Ecclesiastes. In the introduction of his book, Solomon states his big idea—his thesis statement:

All things are wearisome,
more than one can say.
The eye never has enough of seeing,
nor the ear its fill of hearing. (Ecclesiastes 1:8)

Metaphorically he is saying that his eyes never saw enough and his ears never heard enough. And even though we have it all, the life of excess will never satisfy.

Solomon truly "had it all." He was the son of a king, so he inherited a kingdom. But he took the kingdom he inherited to a whole new level, and under his leadership he expanded the kingdom beyond his wildest expectations. One of his greatest accomplishments was the building of the temple that his father David wanted to build. But God told David that Solomon would have that privilege. It took Solomon seven years to build the temple and it was magnificent. After dedicating the temple to God, he began to build his own palace. Solomon's palace was twice the size of the temple, and it took him twice as long to build.

And even though in his early years of leadership he had very humbly asked God for wisdom, as he used that wisdom to expand his kingdom, he grew more and more empty. The story of Solomon is the sad story of the passionate king who showed so much promise. He wrote over 3,000 proverbs and ended up breaking most of them with reckless abandon. Look at what he had.

- Wealth (1 Kings 10:10-25) Silver was made as common as stones (v. 27).

- Power (1,400 chariots, 12,000 horses—1 Kings 10:26)

- Sex (700 wives, 300 concubines—1 Kings 11:3)

- Peace ("For he ruled over all the kingdoms west of the Euphrates River, from Tiphsah to Gaza, and had peace on all sides."—1 Kings 4:24)

Solomon's kingdom seemed to be a success. In history Israel would look at the years of Solomon as the fruitful, glory years. It was a time of prosperity and good times. But Solomon's own family devastated it. His two sons shattered what he had taken 40 years to build. Rehoboam followed his father's lifestyle of excess and became a fool. Jeroboam led a rebellion against his father and divided the kingdom—a kingdom that would not be united until the coming of Jesus Christ.

And when Solomon wrote the conclusion of his book, he addressed his remarks to the young. He said,

> *Remember your Creator*
> *in the days of your youth,*
> *before the days of trouble come*
> *and the years approach when you will say,*
> *"I find no pleasure in them." (Ecclesiastes 12:1)*

And his last words in this book are insightful. He has tried everything from earthly wisdom, to wealth, pleasure, things, sexuality, learning, and success and all of it has left him empty. After all of that he finally sums up his search for fulfillment by saying:

> *[13]Now all has been heard;*
> *here is the conclusion of the matter:*
> *Fear God and keep his commandments,*
> *for this is the duty of all mankind.*
> *[14]For God will bring every deed into judgment,*
> *including every hidden thing,*
> *whether it is good or evil. (Ecclesiastes 12:13-14)*

In essence Solomon is saying to us, "I've done it all, and there is only one thing that is constant and upon which you can depend your entire life: Fear God and keep his commandments."

CLOSING

Justin seemed to have it all, but he didn't. He achieved everything seemingly possible…but still felt empty.

How about you? What drives you?

The only way you can find fulfillment is in your passionate desire for a relationship with God. God has given you certain gifts. They might be musical or athletic. He may have given you artistic ability or leadership ability.

The question is: What are you going to do with these abilities? You can use these God-given abilities to honor God...or to try to build your own success. But you see how that turns out. Remember the stories of Justin and Solomon.

Let's pray.

SMALL GROUP QUESTIONS

1. **Around the Circle:** If your school yearbook voted "most likely to..." for every student in your class, how would your friends finish that sentence for you?

2. **Around the Circle:** Finish the sentence: I would be much happier if I only had ...

3. **Ask Just a Few:** What are some of the common things that people pursue for happiness?

4. **Ask Just a Few:** Are they happy when they get these things? For how long?

As King Solomon looked back on his empty life, he wrote the book of Ecclesiastes; and in the introduction of his book in chapter one he shares the theme of the book:

All things are wearisome,
more than one can say.

The eye never has enough of seeing,
nor the ear its fill of hearing. (Ecclesiastes 1:8)

5. **Ask Just a Few:** Why do you think a king who has everything (money, sex, power...name it) would say, "All things are wearisome"?

6. **Ask Just a Few:** Do you think this perspective is ever shared by rich and powerful people today? Explain.

When Solomon wrote the conclusion of his book, he addressed his remarks to the young. He said,

Remember your Creator
in the days of your youth,
before the days of trouble come
and the years approach when you will say,
"I find no pleasure in them." (Ecclesiastes 12:1)

Then Solomon tells us to fear God's commandments. In essence Solomon is saying to us, "I've done it all, and there is only one thing that is constant and upon which you can depend your entire life: Fear God and keep his commandments."

7. **Ask Just a Few:** Do you find this advice credible, from a man who had it all? Explain.

8. **Ask Just a Few:** God gives us plenty of gifts and abilities in life. What are some ways that we can use these gifts to honor him, not to build our own success?

9. **Around the Circle:** What is one thing you can do this week to honor God with what you've been given? How can I, as your youth group leader, help you do that?

TALK 14
TITLE: THE MIRACLE OF FORGIVENESS

TOPIC: Forgiveness

BIG IDEA: Because of Jesus' death on the cross we can experience forgiveness and forgive others.

SCRIPTURE

> Jesus said, "Father, forgive them, for they do not know what they are doing." (Luke 23:34)

PARTICULARS

Revenge is a popular theme in movies, TV shows, and best-selling books. This story, text and application, however, are about forgiveness, peace, and mercy.

This is another example of a talk that could be used in both Outreach and Spiritual Growth venues. The talk encourages believers to forgive, yet at the same time presents an amazing opportunity to invite unbelievers to experience the forgiveness Christ offers. So feel free to use it in either venue.

The subject matter is a little dark—be warned. But such is the reality of sin in this world. And God's love shines brightly in such dark places.

STORY

It's hard to forgive others when they're mean to us.

It's even more difficult to forgive when people are downright cruel.

As for Margaret Achiro's story...forgiveness would seem a near impossibility.

It was a warm day in Uganda when Margaret and her three friends worked in their garden. A slight breeze gave the foursome comfort as they dedicated themselves to the task at hand. But the stillness of the morning was about to be broken by an evil beyond what many of us can fathom.

A group that ironically called themselves "The Lord's Resistance Army" (the LRA) ventured on Margaret's property to loot and assert their power. The rebel soldiers were known for their brutal raids where they would capture children, stealing food and supplies along the way. But today, the soldiers decided that stealing was not enough. The soldiers dragged the four of them away from their garden and began chopping up Margaret's friends' bodies into pieces with machetes.

Margaret watched the slaughter for about 30 minutes as they killed her friends. Five months pregnant, she prayed to God to save her life for the sake of her baby and so that her other children wouldn't have to try to survive in this cruel world without a mother.

Her prayers were answered and her life was spared. The adult commander noticed that Margaret was pregnant and believed that it would bring bad luck to the LRA to kill a pregnant woman, so he ordered three of the kids he had abducted from earlier lootings to cut her lips, cut off her nose and her ears, and leave her to die. The LRA commander felt that if she died on her own, they would not be responsible for her death.

Fortunately Margaret was found and rushed to a local hospital where she received first aid. She survived, and in three months gave birth to her son, James. But she was so disfigured by the child soldiers that her husband abandoned her. Margaret said that he no longer considered her beautiful, so he left her alone with one of her children.

Alone, disfigured, and helpless, Margaret cried out to God for comfort.

God continued to answer Margaret's prayers as she was brought to the World Vision Children of War Rehabilitation Center where she was given medical, psychological, and spiritual help. She received reconstructive surgery, trauma support, counseling, and vocational seamstress training.

It was a long, hard road to health, and she seemed to be doing well... until that day she saw the three children who had disfigured her.

Those visiting the World Vision Center in northern Uganda that day were shocked as the scarred, disfigured woman literally screamed and cursed at a group of kids walking through the center. Chaos ensued as she lunged toward them like a wounded lioness protecting her cubs.

The kids who had been forced to mutilate her were rescued from captivity, and they also had been brought to the World Vision Center for counseling and rehabilitation. Margaret was livid. How could she live in the same place as these evil children? The counselors at the center explained to Margaret that they would deal with the children, but she was the only one who could free herself from the torture chamber of bitterness.

Margaret's biggest struggle wasn't physical anymore. It was internal. Margaret's bitterness and anger were eating her from the inside out. She knew that freedom from this bondage would require forgiving the children. As much as the images of them hurting her haunted her memories, she knew that forgiving them would be her only way to completely heal.

It took time, but finally Margaret and the children came together to live in harmony.

Just as Margaret and the children had reconciled, she ran into the leader of the LRA who had given the cruel orders to mutilate her, changing her life forever. The rage and the pain returned in a second. She went wild again, threatening to attack him to prove that she could defend herself this time. The LRA leader wouldn't admit that he was the same commander. This enraged Margaret even more. Her instincts told her to fight him and make him pay for what he had done to her.

Time passed and the anger and hatred wore on Margaret's soul. In time the man admitted his wicked acts and asked for forgiveness. Margaret made peace.

But Margaret's journey of peace-making and reconciliation didn't stop there. Her husband eventually came to the same center and was also counseled. He also asked to be forgiven. In time Margaret forgave him as well, letting go of all resentment, even though he left her when she needed him the most.

Margaret said, "I have forgiven everyone including my husband. I realized it must have been hard on them, too. The children had to choose between death and life, the commander implementing orders given to him, and my husband had to choose between having to live with a woman without lips and a nose and walking out. That is life. But my stay here has really changed my attitude about everything. I find it easier to accept my situation now and focus on the best."

For more than 20 years the Lord's Resistance Army and its leader, Joseph Kony, a monster who claimed to be the son of God, ruled northern Uganda. During his reign of terror he kidnapped more than 38,000 children who were forced at gunpoint to commit murder, rape, and acts of cannibalism. The children he did not kill were forced to become the child soldiers of the LRA. He forced them to use machetes to kill their own brothers and sisters because bullets were too valuable to squander on killing the Ugandans. The girls, often just 12 and 13, were gang raped and forced to become sex slaves. During the 20-year period 1.5 million people were driven from their land and forced to live in camps.

Margaret was just one of the individuals who lived under this reign of terror. Now she is not only free from living under such an evil tyrant... she's free from the torture of bitterness. Forgiveness is the key that unlocked that door.

TRANSITION STATEMENT

The miracle of forgiveness isn't natural as it goes against our instincts. Revenge is a much tastier theme in today's movies, TV shows, and bestsellers. Let's face it: we love to see the bad guys get a dose of the treatment that they dished out for years.

APPLICATION AND SCRIPTURE

The Bible, however, has a different message. It's because of Jesus that we can experience forgiveness and forgive others. Jesus tells us to love our enemies. He tells us to "turn the other cheek." Even while dying his painful and cruel death on the cross, Jesus prayed to his father,

"Father, forgive them, for they do not know what they are doing." (Luke 23:34)

I don't know about you, but I wouldn't have blamed Jesus if he had ordered some lightning bolts to strike some people when they were crucifying him. We don't expect a person who is being nailed to a cross to offer forgiveness to the people who condemned him to die or to his executioners. That is what Jesus did for us.

I want us to focus on one word of his prayer—*them*. When he prayed, "Father, forgive them, for they do not know what they are doing," who was included? Our first reaction is that he was referring to the people who were there—religious leaders who condemned him, the mob who yelled "crucify him," the soldiers who carried out their orders and killed him, the disciples who ran. Sure, Jesus included all these sinners in the "them" of the prayer, demonstrating that no one is beyond the reach of God's grace. That's just who Jesus is. He forgave people that others would never forgive. The powerful message of the cross is that he's willing to forgive the worst of sinners. Our first reaction is right on.

But there's more. *Them* included those who weren't there that day.

Them also included some really devoted people like Peter who just got scared. It includes people like a lot of us who mean well, but in a crisis blow it. I can rationalize that I'm not that bad. I'm not the kind of person who would show up at a hanging or crucifixion. I'm not like those people. I'm better than that. However, when I really look at my life, I see a lot of stuff that I wish I hadn't done, or thought, or felt. When I'm really honest, I need forgiveness from others and from God. I am included in the "them." This is where the words of Jesus become very personal.

The prophet Isaiah described the details of Jesus' death in Isaiah 53. In the last verse of that chapter Isaiah said, "For he bore the sin of many, and made intercession for the transgressors." That is an amazing prophecy. Hundreds of years before Jesus died, Isaiah said that when Jesus was killed he would pray for those whose sins he died for. Jesus was praying for us while he was taking on our sins.

Margaret Achiro recognized the power of Christ's death on the cross and his forgiveness. Her life totally changed after she accepted the love of Christ and forgave those who wronged her. She says, "It is no use clinging to hatred. What I realize is that you deprive yourself of peace."

She now goes to bed and wakes up with her mind focused on rebuilding her family's lives.

CLOSING

How about you? Are there people in your life whom you want to repay with revenge? A friend? A teacher? Someone in your family? The problem with revenge and hatred is that it eats at you, rotting you from the inside out, and keeping you from experiencing the miracle of a new beginning. Forgiveness frees you from that pain and releases you from the torture chamber of bitterness.

Forgiveness starts with accepting Christ's death on the cross for our sins. In order to enter a relationship with Christ, we need to recognize our need for Christ's death and accept his forgiveness. We need to recognize our need for God because we have sinned. Romans 3:23 reminds us, "for all have sinned and fall short of the glory of God." God doesn't grade on a curve. We don't receive eternal life because we are better than others or miss eternal life because we are worse. None of us is perfect, and we often feel frustrated and empty because of the stupid things that we do, think, and feel.

The Bible tells us over and over again that Jesus came to earth, not just to teach nice stuff and demonstrate how to live, but to provide us salvation through his death on the cross. Probably the best known verse of Scripture is John 3:16, "For God so loved the world that he gave his one and only Son, that whoever believes in him shall not perish but have eternal life."

You can experience the forgiveness of God right now.

Let's pray.

SMALL GROUP QUESTIONS

1. **Around the Circle:** Share about a time when someone was really mean to you.

2. **Ask Just a Few:** When is forgiveness most difficult?

3. **Ask Just a Few:** How do you feel when someone forgives you?

4. **Ask Just a Few:** How do you feel when you forgive someone?

Jesus doesn't ask us to do anything that he hasn't done for us already. While dying his painful and cruel death on the cross, Jesus prayed to his Father,

"Father, forgive them, for they do not know what they are doing." (Luke 23:34).

5. **Ask Just a Few:** How would that story have changed if Jesus would have used his power to jump off the cross and start kicking butt?

6. **Ask Just a Few:** Do you have someone in your life that you need to forgive right now? What would you feel if you forgave that person?

7. **Around the Circle:** The Bible says that all of us have sinned (Romans 3:23). What would it feel like to have those sins forgiven?

8. **Around the Circle:** Forgiveness is free to anyone willing to put his or her trust in Jesus. Would any of you like to receive that forgiveness right now? (Take the pressure off interested parties by suggesting the group members close their eyes and raise their hands if they're interested in receiving Christ.)

TALK 15
TITLE: IT'S NOT HURTING ANYBODY

TOPICS: Warnings, Consequences, Excuses

BIG IDEA: God provides freedom from the unavoidable consequences waiting for us when we lie to ourselves and justify our actions.

SCRIPTURE

> ⁷Do not be deceived: God cannot be mocked.
> A man reaps what he sows. ⁸Whoever sows to
> please their flesh, from the flesh will reap destruction;
> whoever sows to please the Spirit, from the Spirit
> will reap eternal life. (Galatians 6:7-8)

PARTICULARS

This story is based on a true event that happened in the fall of 2011 in California. The names and small details have been changed for anonymity.

STORY

Jamie Heller always thought she'd get away with it. The fact is, she did get away with it most of the time. Almost every time, in fact. She had the art of "getting away with it" down to a science. But it was only a matter of time before Jamie's actions would catch up with her and she would face the consequences of her decisions.

When Jamie was 22 years old, driving home from her cousin's house on an October Monday night...that time finally arrived.

Some people might blame her parents. Dad left at an early age. Mom tried her best to raise the kids at first, but eventually turned to the bottle. Grandma took custody of the kids for a while, but by then, Jamie and her two brothers were already getting in trouble in school and with the law. Jamie's oldest brother did a year in Juvenile Hall, but Jamie kept getting away with stuff.

When Jamie was just 12, her grandmother caught Jamie and her brother throwing rocks over the cinderblock wall into the speeding traffic on the freeway.

"What in heaven's name are you doing, child?" her grandma howled, catching Jamie mid-throw.

Jamie raised her chin as if she had nothing to worry about: "Just throwing rocks."

Jamie's grandma wasn't having any of it. "Just throwing rocks?!! What kind of answer is that?"

"It's not hurting anybody."

This was Jamie's answer for everything. Even if her actions were hurting someone, Jamie somehow found a way to justify her actions, convincing herself that she wasn't hurting anyone, or that the people being hurt deserved it.

Jamie continued to find trouble wherever she went. Detention didn't bother her, nor did the small hand slaps she received from the police. Jamie didn't even flinch when she was given a DUI. She was a minor, so it wasn't long before she was back behind the wheel again as a young adult.

By the time Jamie was 20, her record was freckled with countless citations. But Jamie hadn't learned her lesson.

After Jamie had a daughter out of wedlock, she began working two jobs to support her daughter. She also began going to school to become a nurse. But her good decisions never seemed to outweigh the bad ones; by age 22 she found herself on parole, with no auto insurance, and driving on a suspended license.

On an October evening in 2011, Jamie left her cousin's house and began driving on the freeway. As she approached her exit, Jamie pulled out her cell phone and began texting a friend. With her head down, she clipped the right side of Richard Baxter's motorcycle, knocking him over. The fall didn't kill him, but when the vehicle following him couldn't swerve in time, it ran over Baxter, killing him instantly.

Jamie's actions had finally caught up with her. Unfortunately she wasn't the only one facing the consequences for her actions this time. She had killed a Navy veteran, and she had dragged other drivers into her nightmare who would be plagued for the rest of their lives with the memory of this tragic night.

Jamie tried to concoct a lie at first, claiming she had a flat tire. But the evidence revealed the truth.

The judge sentenced Jamie with harsh words about her texting, her lying, and her pattern of reckless behavior: "The defendant engaged in reckless and senseless behavior, and now as a result of the incident, a son, a husband, a father, a grandfather, a brother, a brother-in-law, an uncle is dead."

Jamie eventually pleaded no contest and was sentenced for a term not exceeding five years.

Baxter's family shouted through tears in the courtroom, "I hope you never get your license back when you get out of jail!" Baxter's daughter shouted, "I hope you never get another phone. You don't deserve a phone, you don't deserve a car, you don't deserve your freedom...you don't even deserve your life!"

Jamie might have actually heard these words. She wrote an apology letter to all involved saying, "I sit in my cell, and I'm always thinking about what I did, and I lie in bed and mourn for Mr. Baxter and his family and how my careless and stupid acts brought such hardship."

Our actions have consequences.

TRANSITION STATEMENT

Jamie's mantra, "It's not hurting anybody," finally caught up with her. Her life of self-deception had huge consequences and deeply hurt others.

APPLICATION AND SCRIPTURE

The Bible has very strong words for Jamie, and for us when we dupe ourselves into believing the lie that we can do anything we want "as long as no one else gets hurt." It is an easy lie to believe, and we all do it from time to time. Right?

Listen to these words from Galatians 6:7:

Do not be deceived: God cannot be mocked. A man reaps what he sows.

The Greek word that the Apostle Paul uses for *deceived* means to lie to, to con, to cheat, to hoodwink, to defraud, to dupe, or to cheat. Jamie lied to herself, as she needed to find ways to justify her actions. She probably said at times...

- My dad left when I was young.

- My mother was an alcoholic.

- I'm a single mom.

- I'm working two jobs.

- I'm going to school.

- These California laws about texting are stupid.

- I'm a better driver than everyone else.

- The laws are for everyone else, not me.

- It won't happen to me.

- I won't hurt anyone else.

One of the ways that we are duped is to live in a fantasy world where we can do anything we want and it won't affect anyone else. When we believe that lie, we are acting as "god" in our lives. In essence we are saying, "I don't care what the rules of the state are, I'm the master of my own fate. Those rules are for dumb drivers—I'm too cool and have better hand-eye coordination than the average person."

Paul said that when we mislead ourselves in this way we are "mocking God." He uses a Greek word that literally means "to turn up our nose at God." We are actually saying to God, "I am god of my life, and I make up my own rules and it won't affect anyone else."

Paul goes on to say that this kind of self-deception has a consequence that he calls the "harvest." When we plant our own misguided, God-mocking actions, we reap the consequences. Paul doesn't mince any words. He says,

⁷Do not be deceived: God cannot be mocked. A man reaps what he sows. ⁸Whoever sows to please their flesh, from the flesh will reap destruction; whoever sows to please the Spirit, from the Spirit will reap eternal life. (Galatians 6:7-8).

The consequences are huge—destruction. Other Bible translations use "decay and death." People who mock, or turn up their noses at, God's principles face decay and death.

What does Paul mean by "decay and death"?

First, I believe that these words of judgment—decay and death—describe what happened to the Baxter family. Listen again to the judge's reprimand to Jamie about her texting, lying, and pattern of reckless behavior: "The defendant engaged in reckless and senseless behavior, and now as a result of the incident, a son, a husband, a father, a grandfather, a brother, a brother-in-law, an uncle is dead."

And second, Jamie experienced her own feelings of emotional decay and death when sitting in her cell she reflected, "I'm always thinking about what I did, and I lie in bed and mourn for Mr. Baxter and his family and how my careless and stupid acts brought such hardship."

But notice the contrast in the text. Those who follow God's principles and live according to his spirit reap a harvest of blessing. We have a choice—the harvest of God's blessing or the harvest of death and decay.

If we're being honest, this choice is a no-brainer. "Hmmmmm. Let me think. Death and decay, or God's blessing for eternity?"

Duh!

Stop lying to yourself. All actions have consequences, good or bad. God is offering you the choice. Which do you choose?

CLOSING

Do you ever find yourself making excuses to ignore God's principles?

- It won't hurt anyone else.

- These influences don't affect me.

- My parents are old fashioned and don't understand.

- What's the big deal? It's only a little bit dishonest.

- I'll see how close I can get to this sin without actually sinning.

If you are following these excuses of self-deception, remember that there are huge consequences of decay and death. Like Jamie, you might get away with it for a while, but the day of reaping will come.

God can free us from living this lie if we're willing to put our trust in him.

Which do you choose?

Let's pray.

SMALL GROUP QUESTIONS

1. **Around the Circle:** What is your favorite feature on your cell phone?

2. **Ask Just a Few:** Why are the "texting while driving" laws becoming such a big deal?

3. **Ask Just a Few:** In the story, Jamie always convinced herself that her actions weren't hurting anyone, when most of the time they were. Why do we sometimes lie to ourselves like this?

Listen to these words from Galatians 6:7-8:

⁷Do not be deceived: God cannot be mocked. A man reaps what he sows. ⁸Whoever sows to please their flesh, from the flesh will reap destruction; whoever sows to please the Spirit, from the Spirit will reap eternal life. (Galatians 6:7-8)

4. **Ask Just a Few:** Why do you think Paul writes, "Do not be deceived"?

5. **Ask Just a Few:** What does "a man reaps what he sows" mean?

6. **Ask Just a Few:** What are ways we "sow to please our flesh"?

7. **Ask Just a Few:** What did Jamie reap from her actions in the story?

8. **Ask Just a Few:** How do we "sow to please the Spirit"?

9. **Ask Just a Few:** What does the person who sows to please the Spirit get?

10. **Around the Circle:** What is a way that we might be sowing to please our flesh? How can we avoid doing this?

11. **Around the Circle:** How can we pursue sowing to please the Spirit this week? How can I, as your youth group leader, help you do that?

12. **Around the Circle:** Forgiveness is free to anyone willing to put his or her trust in Jesus. Would any of you like to receive that forgiveness right now? (Take the pressure off interested parties by suggesting the group members close their eyes and raise their hands if they're interested in receiving Christ.)

TALK 16

TITLE: RUINED, RESCUED, AND RESTORED

TOPICS: Redemption, Restoration

BIG IDEA: When our lives are a mess, we are wrecked, and we feel like pieces of junk, God is our restorer who is so passionate about us that he paid for our redemption with his own life.

SCRIPTURE

> [18]For you know that it was not with perishable things such as silver or gold that you were redeemed from the empty way of life handed down to you from your ancestors, [19]but with the precious blood of Christ, a lamb without blemish or defect. (1 Peter 1:18-19)

PARTICULARS

I used to have a seminary professor who would say to us when we interpreted parables, "Don't try to make every object, person, or every action of the story mean something." He urged us to find the central idea of that parable. The same is true for most of the stories we tell to illustrate a scriptural point. We don't try to make every aspect of the story mean something; we just use the story to illustrate the Big Idea.

This story is a redemption story. The captivating message is the big idea, "When our lives are a mess and we are wrecked and feel like pieces of junk, God is our restorer who is so passionate about us that he paid for our redemption with his own life."

STORY

It didn't look like much. Rusted and beat up, covered in Georgia clay. At first glance car buffs would have recognized it as a 1969 Dodge Charger . . . but this particular vehicle was so much more.

It was General Lee 1.

This is the true Hollywood story of the original General Lee. It is a story of destruction, rescue, restoration, and redemption. It is the story of the journey of this very special 1969 Dodge Charger, which has gone from being a brand-new car off the lot, a used car, a pop-culture phenomenon, and a wreck buried in Georgia mud, to a painstakingly restored pricy icon of American history. It's the story of a car that Johnny Cash sang about and that Bubba Watson, winner of the 2012 Masters, purchased for $110,000.

In its seven-year star career, the General Lee 1 was the hot, bright orange car with the "Dixie" horn featured in The *Dukes of Hazzard* TV show which ran from 1979 until 1985. In 1978 the General Lee 1 was just a nine-year-old used Dodge Charger with a 383 engine and a torque-flight transmission cruising the freeways of southern California. It had been owned by several people who could have never dreamed of its call to fame and that one day it would be sold for more than $100,000.

Warner Bros. writer-director Gy Waldron wanted to make a new TV series out of his 1975 film *Moonrunners*. But he knew he would have to jazz up the boring stock car used in *Moonrunners*, so he charged the transportation department at Warner Bros. to come up with something cool for Bo and Luke Duke and their cousin Daisy Duke to race around in the TV series. The stock car in *Moonrunners* had been named Traveler after the horse General Robert E. Lee rode during the Civil War, so they decided to name the Dukes' car the General Lee.

Warner Bros. started buying up every '69 Charger in southern California and painting them bright orange.

On November 11, 1978, The *Dukes of Hazzard* pilot episode was filmed on the campus of Oxford College in Georgia. A stuntman raced the General Lee 1 up a dirt ramp and jumped it over a 1974 Monaco cop car, a leap that shot 16 feet high and flew 82 feet across—and it's the now-famous jump scene shown at the end of the opening credits.

Even though the trunk was full of concrete to balance the weight of the engine to keep it from nosing over, the General Lee 1 landed so hard it wrecked the front fenders and bent the floor pan and sills just behind the firewall. After that one jump, it was modified and only used in one more show a few weeks later. Even though, by some estimates, the producers actually wrecked 320 additional General Lees during filming of the TV series, the very first General Lee 1 is the only Lee to appear in every episode of the seven-year run of the show.

The one-jump-scene television career of the General Lee 1 had come to an end. It ended up rotting away in the Georgia clay in a junkyard.

But something happened some 22 years later.

Indianapolis disc jockey Travis Bell took his enthusiasm for The Dukes far beyond mere fandom. He became obsessed with the General Lee 1 and became one of the co-founders of the North American General Lee Fan Club. Although he owned a General Lee replica, he wanted the real thing—the one shown during each episode's credits. Rummaging around the backwoods of Georgia, Bell found the first General Lee—

junked, abandoned, and rotting away. He paid a three-figure price, put it on a trailer, and hauled it back to his home in Indiana.

The restoration process was painful. At first Bell took it to shows, but people kept stealing souvenirs from it. He didn't have the money to invest in the restoration, and it was becoming so stressful to guard and preserve that Bell sold it on eBay for $20,400 to a group of investors from Ohio. The investors soon realized that they had no vision for the restoration of the General, so they put it back on eBay and sold it to an investor from Florida, Martin Murphy, who would finance the restoration under Bell's watchful eye. Finally, almost four years after Travis found the original General Lee in Georgia, the restoration process was complete, costing Murphy about $75,000.

When the restored General Lee 1 was ready for its debut, Travis decided to do it up big. He put it on a trailer and hauled it to the exact spot where it first jumped on the campus of Oxford College in Georgia. And 28 years later to the day of its first flight, November 11, 2006, Travis Bell had his friend, John Schneider—the original Bo Duke himself—drive the car off the trailer.

TRANSITION STATEMENT

So much care was put into the rescue, redemption, and restoration of General Lee 1...and it's just a car.

If only you knew the price that Jesus has invested in your rescue, redemption, and restoration.

APPLICATION AND SCRIPTURE

We, like every brand-new car driven off the showroom floor, are full of promise and expectations. But after miles on the road, dents from people, and a few wrecks from disappointments, our dreams are shattered, and we feel like pieces of junk.

It is at this time that we need to be reminded that we have someone who is passionate about us, our Creator, who made us to be special: For we are God's handiwork, created in Christ Jesus to do good works, which God prepared in advance for us to do. (Ephesians 2:10)

But so often the trials of life mess up that plan.

When I feel like a failure in my Christian life, and I feel like I'm ready for the junkyard, I am reminded of the story of Peter. Jesus loved him and invested in him. Peter must have felt that he was going places. He had been part of miracles, feeding great crowds, with almost three years of executive coaching by the Son of God. Peter had been included in the special three who got to experience things that the other nine disciples didn't get to see. Peter could only imagine that he had a great future in God's kingdom.

But then at the very time when Jesus needed him the most, Peter cursed him and claimed that he didn't even know him. As much as Peter's denial hurt Jesus, the pain that it caused Peter must have been so excruciating. Meeting up with Jesus after the resurrection, Peter must have felt like he was just a piece of junk.

How can people find forgiveness and restoration when they feel that they have failed at a crucial time?

Luckily, the story doesn't end there for Peter. And it doesn't end for us, either. When our lives are a mess, we're wrecked, and we feel like pieces of junk, God is our restorer who is so passionate about us that he paid for our redemption with his own life.

When Jesus seeks out Peter after the resurrection (John 21), Jesus commissions Peter to ministry. In the book of Acts we see Peter is a changed person. He's been restored and is charging ahead as the "rock" that Jesus said he would be. And when he writes his first letter, Peter teaches us that the currency Jesus paid for our redemption wasn't money. And it wasn't paid by an investor or financial conglomerate. It was paid by the blood of Jesus Christ. Blood is a metaphor of life. And Jesus gave his life so that we might be restored.

18For you know that it was not with perishable things such as silver or gold that you were redeemed from the empty way of life handed down to you from your ancestors, 19but with the precious blood of Christ, a lamb without blemish or defect. (1 Peter 1:18-19)

Is it possible to have the realistic hope of a new beginning like the old General Lee 1? The Bible says it certainly is possible. But it won't do just to try to improve this present life. What we need is a whole new life—eternal life. For that, said Jesus, "You must be born again." (John 3:7)

How can we receive this new life? Just as a ruined car cannot remake itself, we cannot restore ourselves, either. This restored life must be received as a gift. "For the wages of sin is death, but the gift of God is eternal life in Jesus Christ our Lord." (Romans 6:23)

CLOSING

If you're feeling rusted, dented, and beat up...know that God wants to rescue, redeem, and restore you. We can't do it ourselves. He's already paid the price. We just need to be willing to let him renovate us.

Are you ready to take that step of faith right now?

Let's pray.

SMALL GROUP QUESTIONS

1. **Around the Circle:** What was your favorite TV show as a kid?

2. **Ask Just a Few:** Have you ever collected anything? What?

3. **Ask Just a Few:** Why did Travis and the other collectors put so much time, effort, and money into the General Lee 1? (Leaders— an answer you might be looking for: Because they saw it as valuable.)

Jesus saw value in us and gave his life so that we might be restored.

¹⁸For you know that it was not with perishable things such as silver or gold that you were redeemed from the empty way of life handed down to you from your ancestors, ¹⁹but with the precious blood of Christ, a lamb without blemish or defect. (1 Peter 1:18-19)

4. **Ask Just a Few:** God bought us or "redeemed us" for a precious price, according to this verse. What was it?

5. **Ask Just a Few:** What does that tell you about your worth, knowing that Jesus not only spilled blood, but gave his life for you?

6. **Ask Just a Few:** Have you ever felt rusted, dented, and beat up? How does it make you feel to know that God values you and wants to renovate you?

7. **Around the Circle:** Are you ready to take that step of faith right now? Forgiveness is free to anyone willing to put his or her trust in Jesus. Would any of you like to receive that forgiveness right now? (Take the pressure off interested parties by suggesting the

group members close their eyes and raise their hands if they're interested in receiving Christ.)

TALK 17

TITLE: WALL GUY

TOPICS: Our Foundation, Resurrection of Christ

BIG IDEA: When you are struggling with questions about the miracles of the Bible, go to the foundational issue—the resurrection.

SCRIPTURE

> [17]And if Christ has not been raised, your faith is futile; you are still in your sins. [18]Then those also who have fallen asleep in Christ are lost. [19]If only for this life we have hope in Christ, we are of all people most to be pitied.
> (1 Corinthians 15:17-19)

PARTICULARS

This story is based on a true story that happened to a friend, and it has served me effectively for years as a parable I tell to help young people understand the importance of our foundation. I'm not a contractor and don't really know the proper terms for much of the home repair analogies; but I find that young people aren't experts in this area either, and seem to like my semantics of "paint guy," "mud guy," and "wall guy." Feel free to use the wording that best fits you.

STORY

Kelli and Dan had been married for a little over a year when they bought their first house. It was everything they wanted. It had three bedrooms, two baths, and a cute little kitchen nook.

Kelli had a knack for decorating, so she immediately began trying different colors of paint on small patches of wall in each room, asking Dan's opinion. Eventually sage was chosen for the master bedroom, burnt orange for the guest bedroom, and a color called "doeskin" for most of the walls throughout the house.

Kelli and Dan did all the painting themselves. They bought rollers, pans, and extension poles. It was actually kind of fun, a sort of rite of passage for the two as homeowners. They even got into a burnt orange paint fight after a case of the late night giggles while painting the guest bedroom, a short battle where Dan ended up wearing more burnt orange than two of the walls.

But eventually the entire house was painted, all the drop clothes were removed, the furniture was set in place, and the wall decorations hung. After hanging the last wedding picture in the hall, the two plopped onto the couch and simply admired their hard work.

"This is our home!" Kelli said with a smile.

"A beautiful one at that," Dan added. "My compliments to the decorator."

A few months later the two of them were in their bed reading. As Kelli flipped a page she looked up at the picture they had carefully hung on the opposite wall. Her eyes caught something white, a speck in a sea of sage near the top of the wall.

"What is that?" Kelli asked.

"What is what?" Dan followed Kelli's gaze to the far wall.

"Up there!" She pointed above the picture to the small white mark near the top of the wall.

Dan finally saw it, too, and stood on the bed to get a closer look: "I can't tell."

He hopped off the bed, grabbed the desk chair, and stood upon it, reaching up to touch the mystery spot. It was a small crack in the paint. The sage paint had cracked, exposing the plaster underneath.

"Huh," Dan wondered out loud. "The paint cracked. We must have not done it thick enough or something."

The next day Dan pulled a small brush, popped open a half-empty can of sage and dabbed a thick gob of sage paint on the crack, being sure to make it thick this time.

"Problem solved."

Three months later Kelli looked up at the same spot and gasped, "No way."

"What?" Dan countered. But then he saw where she was looking and took a peek for himself.

"No! I put so much paint on that. How did it crack?"

They sat there in silence for a few seconds. "Maybe it's the paint," Dan hypothesized.

Kelli smiled. "It was probably the painter," and attacked Dan in tickles.

The next day Dan called a professional painter. Later that week the painter came out, set up a small ladder, and took a good look at the wall.

"I can't help ya."

"What do you mean?" Dan asked.

"I mean, I can't help ya. You don't have a paint problem. You have a mud problem."

Dan squinted and scratched his head. "So what do we do?"

"You call a mud guy."

Dan explained to Kelli what happened. "Paint Guy couldn't fix it. He said we need to call Mud Guy."

"Why?"

"Because it's a mud problem, not a paint problem," Dan retorted. "I don't know. Let me call Mud Guy and let's see what he says."

The next day Dan called out a mud guy. A few days later Mud Guy showed up. He set up a ladder and examined the crack closely. "I can fix this. Simple."

Dan smiled. "That's what I wanted to hear."

Mud Guy slapped some plaster on the wall and made it look pretty. He gave Dan instructions. "Wait at least a day, then paint this."

Dan waited two days and painted it sage once again.

Problem solved.

Three months later Kelli looked up from her book: "No way!"

Dan saw where she was looking and couldn't bear to follow her gaze: "Don't tell me!"

But he looked. Sure enough, a crack. This one looked even bigger.

"Mud Guy obviously didn't know what he was doing. I'll call him again tomorrow and get this thing solved for good."

The next day Dan called Mud Guy. A few days later Mud Guy showed up, set up a small ladder, and examined the crack. This time he took a little more time, then without saying a word, went out to his truck. A minute later he came back in with a level and placed it horizontally against the wall. Then he placed it vertically.

"Aha. No wonder."

"What? What?" Dan asked eagerly.

"No wonder this plaster is cracking. Your wall is all cattywampus."

"Catty-what?"

"It's all cattywampus," Mud Guy repeated. "You need a wall guy."

Dan and Kelli didn't say much to each other that night. They were both too frustrated. This was their dream house, and they were being nickeled and dimed by the crack from their worst nightmares.

The next day Dan called a contractor who did remodels, a guy who understood how to put up the walls in a house. Wall Guy!

A few days later Wall Guy came out to the house. He didn't grab any tools from his truck or even a ladder. He just walked into the bedroom and looked at the crack. "So what happened?"

Dan told him the whole story. He told him how he tried to paint it, but eventually called Paint Guy, who told him that he needed Mud Guy, who told him he needed a Wall Guy. "That's why you're here. You're Wall Guy."

Wall Guy didn't respond. He just stared at the wall. Then he ran his finger down the wall and looked at the hardwood floor. He looked to the left and the right, and then he went out to his truck. A minute later he came in holding a marble.

Dan couldn't wait to see what Wall Guy would do with the marble.

Wall Guy ran his finger down the wall again, all the way to the floor. Then he placed the marble about an inch to the right of where his finger hit the floor. The marble started rolling to the right, gaining speed until it hit the right baseboard with a loud click.

Wall Guy fetched the marble and then retraced his finger down the wall, this time setting the marble about an inch to the left of his finger. The marble began rolling left, gaining speed until it hit the left baseboard with a loud click.

"Aha! That's what I thought."

"What? What?" Dan begged, almost scared to hear the answer.

"It's not your wall," he said. "It's your foundation. Your foundation is weak and sagging on the east and west sides of your house. We could fix your wall a hundred times, and it's going to keep cracking. You need to fix your foundation."

"So I need to call Foundation Guy?"

Wall Guy chuckled. "Yep. You desperately need Foundation Guy. It's time you stop fixing the symptoms and get to the problem.

TRANSITION STATEMENT

Dan and Kelli remind me of so many young people I talk to. They are hung up on various questions about Jesus. Here are some of the common questions I hear:

- Do you really expect me to believe all that hocus pocus that Jesus did miracles?

- Did Jesus really walk on water?

- Did Jesus actually feed over 5,000 people with a few fish and some bread, or is it just some exaggerated story?

- Did Jesus raise his friend Lazarus from the dead? Come on!

Although they are good questions, they are not the foundational question. Once you have answered the foundational question, the others aren't so difficult.

APPLICATION AND SCRIPTURE

When you are struggling with questions about the miracles of the Bible, go to the foundational issue—the resurrection.

Paul tackles the foundational question in 1 Corinthians 15 when he writes:

[17]And if Christ has not been raised, your faith is futile; you are still in your sins. [18]Then those also who have fallen asleep in Christ are lost. [19]If only for this life we have hope in Christ, we are of all people most to be pitied.

The foundational question to all of Christianity is, "Did Jesus really die for our sins and then rise after three days from a sealed tomb guarded by Roman soldiers?" Is this true, or a hoax called Christianity?

Basically Paul is saying that if Christ did not rise from the dead, then we are fools for following him. The resurrection of Jesus Christ is our foundation. When we believe that Christ was killed and then came back to life—that's the biggie. As far as the Christian faith is concerned, the resurrection is the bottom line. It rises or falls on this fact alone.

Paul knows this question is important, so he lists evidence of the resurrection. He says,

⁴He was buried, that he was raised on the third day according to the Scriptures, ⁵and that he appeared to Cephas, and then to the Twelve. ⁶After that, he appeared to more than five hundred of the brothers and sisters at the same time, most of whom are still living, though some have fallen asleep. ⁷Then he appeared to James, then to all the apostles. (1 Corinthians 15:4-7)

Think about it:

- The Romans were experts at crucifixion. They knew what they were doing when they killed Jesus.
- Three days later the tomb was empty. Even Jesus' opponents admitted it. (They made up a rumor that the disciples stole the body.)
- More than 500 people saw the post-crucifixion Jesus in living, breathing flesh. And many of those people were alive telling the story when Paul was writing this letter.
- The fact that cowards who ran away and hid after Jesus was arrested were transformed overnight into people of extraordinary courage is strong evidence for the resurrection. They would go on to turn the world upside-down with Christianity.
- And James, the half-brother of Jesus (who did not believe that Jesus was God when Jesus was doing ministry), was transformed after he saw Jesus die and rise from the dead.

The evidence is overwhelming. If you're interested in more evidence, I can recommend some reading that researches the subject even deeper.

The fact remains: Jesus is alive. One day Jesus was put to death on a cross, and three days later he was walking around again. If Jesus rose from the dead, then everything else falls into place. Did Jesus do miracles? Once you believe the answer to the foundational question, Jesus rose from the dead—the ultimate miracle—then the questions of whether or not he did miracles is rather trivial. If Jesus rose from the dead, do you think he could heal the sick? If he broke the power of death, could he calm an angry sea? Could he feed the multitudes with a few loaves and fish?

The resurrection proves Jesus could do anything. But most important, the resurrection proves that Jesus is who he said he was—the living God. That's what he was killed for in the first place—claiming he was God in the flesh. Well, it turned out to be true.

CLOSING

When you're trying to find answers to questions about the miracles in the Bible, don't waste your time with trivial stuff like Dan and Kelli did, trying to paint and plaster a crumbling wall. Go for the foundational question first—was Jesus who he said he was? And the answer is the foundational answer—the resurrection. Throughout the New Testament, the resurrection stands as the ultimate proof of the truth of the Christian faith. It is our foundation.

Before we pray, let's close our eyes and bow our heads and just think for a moment. Maybe some of you have been messing around trying to fix small cracks when you really need to address the foundational issue. Is Jesus who he said he was? As you sit here thinking, I encourage you to commit to one of two things:

1. If you don't know Jesus and haven't really researched this, commit to seeking the answer to this question. Read the Bible. Open up the book of Luke and read it through. Or ask me and

I can even give you further reading from experts who have researched this thoroughly. But commit to seeking. Jesus said that if you seek, you'll find.

2. Many of you already know the answer in your heart, but you've never responded. If that's you, you can respond in belief right now and tell Jesus, "I'm ready to put my trust in you." We'd love to pray that prayer with you. Grab me or one of the adult leaders after I pray and just say, "I'm ready." We're happy to talk with you about that.

Let's pray.

SMALL GROUP QUESTIONS

1. **Around the Circle:** Describe your dream home.

2. **Ask Just a Few:** What was the problem that Dan and Kelli really had with their house? Why was it silly to keep fixing "symptoms" instead of the real problem?

3. **Ask Just a Few:** Why do you think some people try to answer trivial questions while ignoring the foundational issue: Is Jesus who he said he was?

Paul tackles the foundational question in 1 Corinthians 15:

17And if Christ has not been raised, your faith is futile; you are still in your sins. 18Then those also who have fallen asleep in Christ are lost. 19If only for this life we have hope in Christ, we are of all people most to be pitied.

4. **Ask Just a Few:** What does Paul say would happen if Christ had not been raised from the dead? (v. 17)

5. **Ask Just a Few:** Why would we still be guilty of our sins if Christ didn't rise from the dead?

6. **Ask Just a Few:** What do you think of the evidence we just heard that Jesus died and rose from the dead?

Maybe as you're sitting there, you're in one of three places right now: A) You don't believe Jesus can save you, and you're fine with that; B) You do believe, but you've never put your trust in Jesus and told him that; or C) You believe, and you've already put your trust in Jesus.

7. **Around the Circle:** Which one of these are you? (If they choose B, then you can pray with them right then.)

8. **Around the Circle:** Forgiveness is free to anyone willing to put his or her trust in Jesus. Would any of you like to receive that forgiveness right now? (Take the pressure off interested parties by suggesting the group members close their eyes and raise their hands if they're interested in receiving Christ.)

TALK 18
TITLE: NOBODY'S PERFECT

TOPICS: Mercy, Grace, Forgiveness

BIG IDEA: God's forgiveness gives us a new beginning.

SCRIPTURE

> For the wages of sin is death, but the gift of God is eternal life in Christ Jesus our Lord. (Romans 6:23)

PARTICULARS

I thank my good friend Greg Alderman for sharing this amazing baseball story with me. Greg is a die-hard baseball fan and used this story in one of his sermons. This epic baseball story is more than just a historical account about baseball history, angry fans, or a blown call. It's a story that turned out to be much bigger than the event. It's a story of integrity and grace.

I encourage you to Google pictures of "Jim Joyce crying," and you'll see the pictures we refer to in the story. The pictures are powerful.

Some might be tempted to use this story to talk to believers about "forgiving others." You could definitely use the story for that purpose, but that's not what we did here. The purpose of this talk is to provide a glimpse of God's love and grace that he's extended to us. This is a great salvation message to an outreach audience.

STORY

On June 2, 2010, there had been only 20 perfect games pitched in the more than 130 years of baseball history.

In a perfect game, 27 batters come to the plate, and 27 batters walk away disappointed. A batter might connect with a ball, but the team gets him out. Not only are there no hits, but also there are no walks, no runs, and no errors.

It's a pitcher's dream!

Then on that particular day in 2010, in the ninth and final inning, Armando Galarraga of the Detroit Tigers was just one out away from pitching the 21st perfect game.

That's when it happened.

ESPN had interrupted their regular programming to announce that the perfect game was in progress in Detroit. The crowd was on the edge of their seats when Galarraga threw one over the plate and batter Jason Donald connected.

Donald hit a ground ball and the throw to first was close, but obvious to everyone that the runner was out. It was obvious to everyone except the most important person, umpire Jim Joyce.

Jim called him safe, and the Detroit fans exploded in anger.

The opportunity for a perfect game was gone.

All around the world ESPN fans couldn't believe what they were seeing. The first baseman of the Detroit Tigers put his hands on his head, the universal sign in baseball that you blew it. Immediately the fans' hands went to their heads. Even Jason Donald, the one who should have been out at first base, put his hands on his head when he heard the umpire call him safe. ESPN showed the Detroit Tigers players and Dave Dembrowski, the general manager of the Tigers, all with their hands on their heads.

To the many who were watching ESPN, and to those on the field and in the stands, they had one thought above all—another famous baseball saying: Kill the umpire!

It was clear to everyone. The runner was out.

As the replay ran over and over again, it got worse. The Detroit Tigers players were going into the clubhouse through the hallway when they saw the replay, and they stormed back out to the dugout and started yelling at the umpire.

But this was baseball, not football. No contesting of plays. No stepping under the curtain to check the video. The call was made, and it couldn't be undone.

It started to dawn on Joyce that maybe he made a bad call. He couldn't understand how, after all, as he was in the perfect position to call the runner safe. He wasn't obstructed in any way. He simply thought the runner beat the throw—that was it. End of story.

But as he was going into the hallway with the umpires, he turned to the crew chief Darrel Cousins and asked, "Did I blow the call? Did I kick it?" Cousins was silent. At that moment Joyce knew. He knew without looking that he had messed up. After a moment Cousins looked up at him and said, "Jimmy, I'm so sorry, but from my angle I thought he was out."

True baseball fans realize how earth-shattering this event was; a perfect game is so rare that it's mind-blowing to baseball fans. After more than 385,000 games played in the history of baseball, only 20 were perfect games. It's one of the rarest things in all sports, in fact.

Later that night Joyce reflected on the game and said to himself, "I totally blew it." As he thought about what it was to pitch a perfect game, a phrase came to mind.

No blemishes.

He thought, *A perfect game has no blemishes—no hits, no walks, no errors.* Jim began to recognize that he had done the unthinkable; he had put a blemish on something that otherwise would have been perfect. He knew better than anyone else what that meant, and how bad it was to have blown that call. What's worse is that he came to the horrible recognition that what he'd done could not be undone. He wished he could wake up, and it would all be a dream. He wished that somehow it could be fixed. But it couldn't. There was nothing he could do to change the call. It couldn't be changed.

To add insult to misery, sportscasters and baseball people all over the country were repeatedly describing Joyce's call as the worst call in Major League Baseball history—a bit of an overstatement, as there have been a ton of bad calls in the last century...just few with such historical ramifications.

Joyce was not only being accused of making the worst call in the history of baseball, but also he had to live with the fact that he had robbed someone of being a part of baseball history. A lot of baseball fans can name most of those pitchers who have thrown perfect games. Armando Galarraga wouldn't be in that list.

Joyce was feeling the enormous weight of living with this one huge mistake.

But there is a strange twist to this story. While everyone else was upset at the wrong that was done, the one who was robbed just smiled.

On his way back to the mound after the call, Armando literally smiled.

When the reporters surrounded him at his locker immediately after the game and asked him questions, he smiled. Week after week, day after day, anytime anybody asked him about it, his first reaction was a smile.

But reporters kept putting a mic in front of his face and asking the same question. "How do you feel being robbed of your perfect game because of Jim Joyce's bad call?"

The pitcher Armando smiled and said, "Nobody's perfect."

Nobody's perfect!

It was his smile and his words that changed everything. He showed everyone else how to act in this situation before the following day's game.

In baseball tradition, before the game the managers meet at home plate with the home plate umpire and exchange lineup cards. As the scheduled home plate umpire (the four-person umpire crews rotate their "positions" each game), Jim Joyce would have to be at that meeting. He would have to walk out on that same field where his history-making bad call happened and meet with the managers of both teams.

How would he do that?

To make it worse, the Tigers, rather than sending out their manager, sent Galarraga to home plate with the lineup card. Joyce would have to face Galarraga.

Everyone watched as the pair met on the field. No one could hear what they were saying, but as Armando gave Joyce the lineup card, he patted him on the shoulder.

What a picture.

As the two men stood together, Armando had his hand on Joyce's shoulder. Joyce, a big strong man, fought back tears.

That picture tells the story. It's a picture of integrity, grace, and forgiveness.

TRANSITION STATEMENT

Have you ever had that feeling when you realized what you had done could not be fixed? You blew it, the weight of it hits you, and you just want to shrivel up into the fetal position, sucking your thumb? Well, the story wasn't over for Joyce when he messed up—and the story isn't over for you if you've ever felt the weight of your mistakes...your blemishes.

APPLICATION AND SCRIPTURE

The Bible has a unique way of describing the reality of blemishes. Romans 3:23 says:

> For all have sinned and fall short of the glory of God.

God's standard is perfect. God has no blemishes. God doesn't make mistakes. But we are not perfect. We make mistakes. We do things that upset people. We do things at times that are hard to live with. We have blemishes.

The Apostle Paul, writing in Romans 6:23, says that the consequence of those blemishes is death:

For the wages of sin is death, but the gift of God is eternal life in Christ Jesus our Lord.

Those blemishes lead to a living death of the soul. That's what Joyce probably felt like. The wages of sin is death, and the payment for a mistake is a living death.

For Joyce, it seemed as though nothing could be healed. He had made a bad call with arguably the worst ramification in baseball history. But then something happened—something no one could have anticipated.

Armando smiled.

By his smile he showed the world the power of love, dignity, forgiveness and, most importantly, life. That is what forgiveness is—a new beginning.

This is a picture of what God is all about. God smiles on us, even when we sin. God does not turn his back on us. God loves us even though we are unlovable and unforgivable.

The Bible tells us that even though the wages of sin is death, the gift of God is eternal life through Jesus Christ (Romans 6:23). We can have life again. God has smiled on us. We, like Jim Joyce, realize that we are at a place where we need forgiveness, but we don't know what to do with it.

Can you imagine what Joyce would have done had it not happened this way? What Joyce did seemed unforgivable, but what Galarraga did was a picture of the divine gift of life. With his smile and pat on Joyce's shoulder, Armando gave Jim new life, in effect saying, "the past is over... let's start a new game."

Joyce's ability to move on in his personal and professional life is due in large part to the fact that he admitted he blew it—but even more important than his confession of wrong is the way Galarraga handled everything.

And now they have a relationship. They've spoken about the game and the call together and have won many admirers for their courage, tenderness, strength, sportsmanship, and humanity. They've now cowritten a book appropriately titled, *Nobody's Perfect.*

Paul says the gift of life is in Jesus Christ. The question you might have is how to receive this gift. Paul tells us:

If you declare with your mouth, "Jesus is Lord," and believe in your heart that God raised him from the dead, you will be saved. (Romans 10:9)

Are you ready to do that?

CLOSING

This baseball game will be remembered by so many people, not because it was almost a perfect game but because of what happened afterward. It's remembered because of the way the participants reacted and acted during that whole situation. To many baseball fans, one of the heroes of the game is now Armando Galarraga.

When the weight of it all sets in and the grim reality of the world we live in hits us with full force, Jesus comes to us with a smile—a smile full of love and grace. He will put a hand on our shoulders to show us the way through it all. Even though we've messed up, God goes a giant step further...and is able to fix it! Through Christ there is forgiveness. With Christ there is new life for those who put their trust in him, and that's what a relationship with Jesus is all about.

Let's pray.

SMALL GROUP QUESTIONS

1. **Around the Circle:** Share your favorite food item that you like to buy when you're at a baseball game, another athletic event...or even a movie.

2. **Ask Just a Few:** Can you think of a time when you messed up, and you knew you messed up? What happened?

3. **Ask Just a Few:** What is the best way to respond when you mess up and everyone knows you messed up?

We all mess up. Paul says this in the book of Romans:

For all have sinned and fall short of the glory of God. (Romans 3:23)

4. **Ask Just a Few:** According to the verse, who has sinned?

5. **Ask Just a Few:** Who does "all" include? (Does it include you and me?)

Paul goes on to tell us the result of sin:

For the wages of sin is death, but the gift of God is eternal life in Christ Jesus our Lord. (Romans 6:23)

6. **Ask Just a Few:** What are the wages or results of sin?

7. **Ask Just a Few:** What does Christ Jesus offer as a free gift to us?

Paul says that the gift of life is in Jesus Christ. The question you might have is how to receive this gift. Paul tells us:

If you declare with your mouth, "Jesus is Lord," and believe in your heart that God raised him from the dead, you will be saved. (Romans 10:9)

8. **Around the Circle:** Are you ready to do that right now? Forgiveness is free to anyone willing to put his or her trust in Jesus. Would any of you like to receive that forgiveness right now? (Take the pressure off interested parties by suggesting the group members close their eyes and raise their hands if they're interested in receiving Christ.)

TALK 19
TITLE: SOMEBODY UP THERE IS LOOKING OUT FOR ME

TOPIC: God Reveals Himself to Us

BIG IDEA: Life is more than just "coincidences."

SCRIPTURE

> ¹The heavens declare the glory of God;
> the skies proclaim the work of his hands.
> ²Day after day they pour forth speech;
> night after night they reveal knowledge.
> ³They have no speech, they use no words;
> no sound is heard from them.
> ⁴Yet their voice goes out into all the earth,
> their words to the ends of the world.
> (Psalm 19:1-4)

PARTICULARS

I use this amazing true story as an example of General Revelation—how God reveals himself to us in ways that make us take notice and respond by saying, "There's something much more to life than just coincidence. There must be a God."

But the story doesn't answer the question, "Who is that God?"

When we begin seeing God in our everyday lives, we need to take the next step and discover who he is by looking in the Scriptures. Psalm 19 points us to both the general revelation of God in nature, and the special revelation of God in the Bible and Jesus Christ. (Although I don't use those fancy theological terms in this talk.)

STORY

When Larry Hicks was driving home from work, he was thinking about taking his wife, Donna, to a movie. But by the time he got home he wasn't in the mood anymore, so they decided to have a quiet evening at home.

The quiet evening never happened. Larry and Donna were thrust into an experience that changed their lives forever.

It began as they sat down to watch the evening news in their home at Palos Verdes Lake, near Troy, Alabama. The sound of a low flying small plane caught their attention as it passed their house. Larry looked outside and saw a plane flying close to the shoreline of the lake. The moment he looked, Larry saw the plane hit the support cables of the nearby power lines, flip over and crash into the lake.

Larry's instincts kicked in. He immediately was out the door yelling to his wife, "Call 911!"

Larry was not your ordinary guy. He was a 52-year-old retired Marine sergeant major who was now working as a conservation enforcement officer for the state of Alabama. But it was Larry's past training that would make all the difference in the events that were about to happen.

During the Vietnam War Larry was stationed at the Marine Corps station in Iwakuni, Japan, undergoing a special intensive Search and

Rescue program. When an officer observed Larry's muscular physique and his weight-training routine, he felt that Larry would be a natural.

And he was.

The training for this special Search and Rescue program was specifically directed toward saving pilots who had crashed their planes into water. In two and a half months Larry learned how to get pilots out of planes that had crashed upside down.

It was this training that kicked in that evening as Larry headed for the wrecked plane.

Larry's brother had left a 14-foot aluminum boat with an electric trolling motor at the lake to go fishing. While Donna made the 911 call, Larry commandeered the boat toward the aircraft, which was upside down in the lake, about 100 yards from shore.

When he arrived at the plane, the engine was hot and smoking. High-octane aviation fuel was floating all around the crash site.

He tied the boat to the plane as he climbed on the back half of the aircraft and the broken wing sticking out of the water. Knowing the plane could blow up, Larry dove into the murky water in search of the pilot. During the first dive Larry ran out of air, but on the second dive he could feel his way through the cloudy waters, finding the back of a man's neck. He came up for air again, and the third time down he found the pilot's seatbelt. It happened to be one he recognized.

Larry's training—"Locate Pilot, Extract Pilot"—took over. His actions were second nature. He pulled the pilot from the plane and swam to the surface.

Larry then noticed the pilot was bleeding through the nose and mouth—and not breathing. Bones were sticking through the pilot's legs (i.e., compound fracture), and his feet were facing backward.

Larry's conclusion was that the pilot had drowned. But Larry didn't give up.

Donna's 911 call brought the police, who were onshore by the time Larry pulled the pilot up on the wing sticking above the water. As the rescue team headed toward the wreckage in a rescue boat, Larry used a modified Heimlich maneuver under the pilot's ribs to try and get the water out of his lungs. Using CPR, Larry got the pilot breathing again. Larry hung on to the plane's wing with his left hand, supported the pilot on his chest, and used his right hand to keep his head above the water.

Feeling the stinging sensation from aviation fuel that was burning off his skin, Larry was in great pain.

The rescue team used their boat to float the pilot and Larry to shore and immediately rushed both of them to the Troy hospital. It wasn't until Larry was released from the hospital with gasoline burns on his upper body that he heard that the person whose life he had just saved was the celebrity Jack Roush, NASCAR and Winston Cup car owner since 1988.

The millionaire known for the Roush Mustang was celebrating his 60th birthday by borrowing a close friend's Air-Cam plane for a spin near Troy, Alabama. He didn't remember anything about the crash from the time of the accident until he woke up at the hospital. He inhaled water and gasoline and suffered head injuries, rib fractures, a collapsed lung, compound fractures to his left leg, and broken ankles.

Six days after the accident, as Roush was sitting in his hospital bed on the telephone running his business, he invited Larry and Donna to be flown to the hospital to visit him, and gifts to the Hicks started to come, from clothes and tools to free trips to the races. Six weeks later, Larry and Donna were in Delaware, next to Roush as his guests at the Dover International Speedway watching Roush's Winston Cup racing team.

Larry was recognized with many honors as a result of his heroic rescue of Roush, including the Marine Corps Medal for Heroism, the Carnegie Medal for Heroism from the Carnegie Foundation, the Kiwanis International Robert P. Connelly Medal of Heroism, and the Society of the Sons of the American Revolution Medal for Heroism. The story of the rescue appeared in *People* magazine, and Larry and Jack made the cover of *NASCAR Illustrated*.

When most people hear the account of the events from the evening of April 19, they remark something to the effect of, "There's no doubt that a Higher Power was at work in Jack Roush's incredible rescue."

Think of all the "what ifs" that occurred. Were they just coincidences or something more?

- What if the Air-Cam had hit the high tension power lines and gone down in flames instead of just hitting the support wires?
- What if it had crashed on the ground or hit a tree in the underwater stump field where it landed?
- What if Larry and Donna had gone to a movie that evening?
- What if Larry hadn't heard the plane?
- What if Larry's brother hadn't left the boat ready to go?

Or the most glaring question:

- What if Larry had not been among that small percentage of people with the special knowledge to save a pilot in an upside-down plane that had crashed in water?

TRANSITION STATEMENT

Those are a lot of coincidences. Those "what ifs" cause us to pause and consider the possibility that there must be a God out there. Larry Hicks,

Jack Roush and all who hear their story at some time must have said, "I wonder if somebody up there is looking out for us."

Many of us have seen evidence of God. The question is: What do we do with it?

APPLICATION AND SCRIPTURE

In Psalm 19 David uses the stars in the sky and the sun as a specific testimony of nature that shouts out to us, "There is a God."

> *¹The heavens declare the glory of God;*
> *the skies proclaim the work of his hands.*
> *²Day after day they pour forth speech;*
> *night after night they reveal knowledge.*
> *³They have no speech, they use no words;*
> *no sound is heard from them.*
> *⁴Yet their voice goes out into all the earth,*
> *their words to the ends of the world.*

But why is it that people do not get this message? Why is it that when people see the stars and the sun they totally miss the message and instead of worshiping the creator, God, they often end up worshiping the sun?

The reason is that the witness of God's goodness does not answer questions such as, "If God exists, where is this being?" or "If God exists, does God even care about me?"

The miracles and witness of nature do not answer these kinds of questions. Maybe that's why David goes on, a few verses later, to tell us where some of these answers are:

> *⁷The law of the Lord is perfect,*
> *refreshing the soul.*

The statutes of the Lord are trustworthy,
making wise the simple.
⁸The precepts of the Lord are right,
giving joy to the heart.
The commands of the Lord are radiant,
giving light to the eyes.
⁹The fear of the Lord is pure,
enduring forever.
The decrees of the Lord are firm,
and all of them are righteous.
¹⁰They are more precious than gold,
than much pure gold;
they are sweeter than honey,
than honey from the honeycomb.
¹¹By them your servant is warned;
in keeping them there is great reward. (Psalm 19:7-11)

All this in one simple psalm. It begins with us noticing God's creation, then points us to the place where we can get answers.

David begins the psalm by telling us how God's creation points to "the work of his hands," a message that has penetrated "all the earth." But then David points us to the Scriptures, "the law of the Lord," his "precepts," and his "commands." David tells us that these bring joy to our hearts and light to our eyes, among other things. Then he concludes by saying that the words of God are more precious than gold, sweeter than honey, and a great reward for those who obey them.

Maybe we haven't saved someone from a fiery death or drowning, but we all have experienced the hand of God in our lives. God reveals himself to us through his creation, and in his everyday acts of love and provision. In those things he is saying to us, "Hey, I'm here and I love you."

But then it is up to us to respond by looking in his word and finding out who this God is who's revealing himself to us.

CLOSING

If you're seeking answers to those questions, I want to give you the opportunity to discover the God who is very real. If you are thinking that there must be a God, or a supreme being, or something more to life than just coincidences, we would love the opportunity to show you through the Bible who this God is.

Similarly, if you are a Christian, you want to be able to help those who have questions about the existence of God by pointing out the very specific revelation of God in Jesus Christ. The more we study the Bible the better we can articulate who God is and how we can know him.

Let's pray.

SMALL GROUP QUESTIONS

1. **Around the Circle:** Have you ever witnessed an accident or someone getting hurt? What happened?

2. **Ask Just a Few:** In the story, name as many of the "what ifs" that you can. (What if the plane hit the power lines, what if the plane hit something solid instead of crashing in the water, what if Larry and Donna had gone to a movie that night, what if Larry hadn't heard the plane, what if Larry's brother hadn't left the boat, etc.)

3. **Ask Just a Few:** Do you think there was more than coincidence here?

4. **Ask Just a Few:** Have you ever wondered if there is more to life than what you see...and if there is a God "up there"?

In the psalm we just heard, David began by telling us how he sees God in "the work of his hands" or creation. Then David tells us that God's word is where we can get some of the answers to questions we might have.

5. **Ask Just a Few:** How come some people see God in creation but never dig for answers?

6. **Ask Just a Few:** What are some reasons that people might not want to know more about God?

7. **Around the Circle:** If you discovered that God reveals himself not only through his creation, but through his written word...would that be worth reading? Would you like to investigate this further with me for the next few weeks? (Offer to meet weekly and go through the Bible or a book such as *The Case for Faith*.)

8. **Around the Circle:** Forgiveness is free to anyone willing to put his or her trust in Jesus. Would any of you like to receive that forgiveness right now? (Take the pressure off interested parties by suggesting the group members close their eyes and raise their hands if they're interested in receiving Christ.)

TALK 20
TITLE: ESCAPING DEATH

TOPICS: Death, Eternal Life

BIG IDEA: To answer that question of death with confidence, we need to first answer the question of life.

SCRIPTURE

> [25]Jesus said to her, "I am the resurrection and the life. The one who believes in me will live, even though they die; [26]and whoever lives by believing in me will never die. Do you believe this?" (John 11:25-26)

PARTICULARS

Most people are fascinated by magic. But when you get down to it, a magician is simply tricking the audience into believing something that is not true. One of the most gifted magicians of all time was the great Houdini, often trying to escape death. His story is a great illustration to ask two important questions: What is death? What is life?

We dive pretty deep in the Scripture and application of this short talk, even defining a few words from the original text. Remember, short doesn't necessarily mean "shallow." At the same time, I think you'll be able to keep the audience's attention.

(My friend David R. Smith helped me put this talk together, using a story from his free online illustration database, ItsLikeThis.org, an amazing resource for stories and illustrations, organized by topic.)

STORY

He could escape anything. At least, that's what he said.

And most people believed him. After all, they'd seen him break out of handcuffs, chains, straitjackets, water traps, and even coffins. It didn't seem to matter how ensnared he was, Harry Houdini could always get out.

Always.

In fact, Houdini was so good at escaping that he boasted he'd devised a way to escape death.

On Sunday, October 31, 1926, at precisely 1:26 p.m., he finally got the chance to prove it.

Houdini was one of the first real international superstars. Born Erik Weisz in Budapest in 1874, he immigrated to America with his family while still very young. Unlike his father who was a rabbi, Houdini denounced anything involving religion or spirituality and made magic his passion.

At first, the young magician's performances were limited to mere card tricks and other sleight-of-hand ruses. But when he began experimenting with death-defying escape tricks, he gained true notoriety.

In crowded shows around the world, he entertained the masses with his stunts. He mocked various police departments by asking them to handcuff him, only to break free moments later. In fact, his skill in escaping hand shackles led to a famous showdown in 1904 after a master locksmith in England spent five painstaking years building a set of hand-cuffs thought to be inescapable.

Within a few hours Harry "Handcuff" Houdini was free.

Escaping handcuffs was one thing. Escaping death was another. Houdini knew it...and so did his fans. To keep them entertained, Houdini continually escalated the danger in his acts. Many of his nightmarish stunts caused people in the crowd to gasp and even pass out.

One of his most famous stunts was called the Milk Can Escape. Houdini would be handcuffed and then lowered into an oversized milk can that had been filled with water. The top would then be sealed and Houdini had to escape before drowning. This gut-wrenching stunt was a crowd favorite, and thousands upon thousands witnessed it on multiple continents.

All over the world, throngs of people gathered to watch him escape concocted scenarios. One night he might be dangling upside down in a straitjacket, and the next he might be buried alive six feet in the ground.

But the act that caused his fans to swoon the most was the Overboard Box Escape. The stunt entailed Houdini being put in handcuffs and leg irons...and then in a coffin. The wooden box would then be wrapped in chains and weighted down with hundreds of pounds of lead. Finally, the coffin would be pushed over the side of a boat, sinking to the bottom of a body of water...with Houdini trapped inside.

But each time he performed this harrowing stunt, the superstar magician delighted the crowds by bobbing back to the surface after several heart-pounding moments.

Each time Houdini escaped a dangerous trap, his claim to be able to escape death became a little more believable.

But all of these traps were traps that Houdini had devised. He'd practiced them countless times, and mastered the art of illusion.

But death offers no practice sessions, and it isn't fooled by simple tricks and sleight-of-hand.

And Houdini found that out the hard way.

In October of 1926, while on a performance tour through Canada, Houdini developed a severe case of appendicitis. Houdini so greatly underestimated his emergency that he didn't even seek medical help. Instead, as any world-class entertainer would do, he shrugged off the massive pain and continued his shows without interruption.

Eventually, nature took its course: Houdini's appendix ruptured, poisoning his body with toxins.

Still battling weak health, Houdini met a college student named J. Gordon Whitehead after a show in Montreal. The young man approached Houdini and asked the famous magician if it was really true that he could survive any blow to the stomach. The exhausted and ill magician weakly responded that it was true, and before he could brace himself, Whitehead punched Houdini in the stomach several times.

The unexpected bashing only worsened his acute appendicitis. When Houdini arrived in Detroit on October 24, he had a fever of 104 degrees but took the stage anyway.

It would be his last show.

Houdini was immediately taken to Detroit's Grace Hospital, where his wife Bess and several of his siblings would later join him. During the next few days, the mighty Houdini, who had triumphed over every peril in life, thrashed in excruciating pain on the brink of death.

On Saturday, October 30, Houdini squirmed on his deathbed with his surgeon, Dr. Kennedy, at his side. The famed magician and the doctor talked about magic, spiritualism, and related topics while the physician monitored his patient's health.

Showing considerable vulnerability at one point in the conversation, Houdini turned to Kennedy and confessed, "Doctor, you know, I always wanted to be a surgeon, but I never could. I have always regretted it."

Kennedy was stunned. "Why, Mr. Houdini, that is one of the most amazing statements I have ever heard. Here you are, the greatest magician and the greatest entertainer of your age. You make countless thousands of people happy. You have an unlimited income, and you are admired and respected by everybody, while I am just an ordinary dub of a surgeon trying to struggle through life."

Houdini looked squarely at Kennedy and whispered, "Perhaps those things are true, Doctor, but the difference between me and you is that you actually do things for people. I, in almost every respect, am a fake."

The following day—on Halloween, no less!—Houdini died.

The world gasped when they heard the news. But they also remembered his claim that he could escape death.

Did he really die...or was it just another act?

Could he really come back to life?

For days—and in some cases, weeks—newspaper headlines were filled with updates on the story. It was widely known that Houdini, before dying, had established a secret phrase known only to him and his wife, Bess. The coded message was simply, "Rosabelle, believe," a phrase that harkened back to the very first show they ever performed together. If Houdini could return from the grave and cheat death, he would prove it to Bess—and the world—by uttering the secret phrase.

Several psychics and mediums came forward and claimed to have contacted Houdini, but none of them could reveal the secret message.

Finally, Arthur Ford, a psychic who claimed to be a pastor, promised Bess that he and his associates could contact Houdini via medium and séance. With thousands and thousands of practicing psychics during that era, Ford's claim seemed as quacked as the others. But Ford argued he could deliver the secret message known only to Bess.

In dramatic fashion, with members of the press present, Ford conjured up the spirit of Harry Houdini. In painstaking detail, he repeated the silent conversation that Houdini was having with his wife. Down to the detail, everything was verified, including the secret message, "Rosabelle, believe."

The next day, the world was taken by headlines that screamed, "Houdini Breaks Chains of Death!" and "Houdini Speaks from the Grave!"

There was just one problem. The whole event was as fake as Houdini's performances. Within days, it was revealed that the entire event was a sham, and Bess eventually owned up to her deceit.

With each passing year, psychics and mediums continued to try to contact Houdini. With each passing year, they failed.

Finally, on October 31, 1936, exactly a decade after Houdini's death, Bess employed even more spiritualists in an attempt to contact her dead husband one last time. On top of the famous Knickerbocker Hotel in Los Angeles, with 300 people watching and millions across the country listening by radio, Bess and other mediums tried to raise Houdini's spirit.

They didn't.

At the end of the séance, her manager and partner, Edward Saint, turned to Bess. "Mrs. Houdini, the zero hour has passed. The 10 years are up. Have you reached a decision?"

"Yes," Bess said sadly. "Houdini did not come through. My last hope is gone. I do not believe that Houdini can come back to me—or to anyone."

Harry Houdini, the man who'd escaped from the most amazing traps ever devised, had failed to escape death.

Sources: http://itslikethis.org/?p=2917, http://itslikethis.org/?p=3284

TRANSITION STATEMENT

What's your plan to escape death?

To answer that question of death with confidence, we need to be able to answer a much more important question about life: "What is life?"

So let's talk about the real question concerning death, "What is life?"

APPLICATION AND SCRIPTURE

The Gospel writer John gives us an answer to that question in a very familiar story from the life of Jesus. His very close friend Lazarus had died. Listen to what happens when Jesus arrives at the Jewish wake four days after Lazarus' passing.

[17]On his arrival, Jesus found that Lazarus had already been in the tomb for four days. [18]Now Bethany was less than two miles from Jerusalem, [19]and many Jews had come to Martha and Mary to comfort them in the loss of their brother. [20]When Martha heard that Jesus was coming, she went out to meet him, but Mary stayed at home.

[21]"Lord," Martha said to Jesus, "if you had been here, my brother would not have died. [22]But I know that even now God will give you whatever you ask."

[23]Jesus said to her, "Your brother will rise again."

[24]Martha answered, "I know he will rise again in the resurrection at the last day."

[25]Jesus said to her, "I am the resurrection and the life. The one who believes in me will live, even though they die; [26]and whoever lives by believing in me will never die. Do you believe this?" (John 11:17-26)

Martha was the sister of Lazarus, one of Jesus' best friends. Jesus used to hang out with Lazarus in Bethany. The home of Martha, Mary, and Lazarus was as close to a home as Jesus ever had.

Martha was really hurting and angry because she believed in her heart that Jesus could have healed Lazarus. In her anger, when she heard that Jesus was outside their home, she got up and ran out to meet him and let him have it: "What took you so long, Jesus? If you had come on time, he wouldn't have died. But I also know that you have the power through your heavenly Father to bring him back from the dead—right now." When Jesus responded with the words, "Don't worry, Martha, he will rise again," those words did not comfort her. She was so heated at Jesus' supposedly theological answer that she basically said, "Hey, I know he will rise again in the future, but I want him here with us now. Do your thing—bring him back now." It was the cry of anger and grief.

When Jesus responded to Martha's anger, he got to the issue of death and life, answering our question, "What is life?" We miss the answer when we read the text in English, but Martha would understand. He spoke her language, and he chose a word very carefully so that she would know what life and death with Jesus is all about.

The New Testament uses two Greek words that translate to the English word "life"—*bios* and *zoe*. And there is all the difference in the world between them!

Bios is the life we receive from our parents. Although it can be a good and fulfilling life, it runs down and decays. *Bios* is life that dies. Houdini had only a *bios* life. He had a life of entertaining people. He accomplished personal goals. But in the end, he died. His *bios* life ran out. It was the only life he knew.

But Jesus didn't use the word *bios* in this passage. Jesus used the other word for "life"—*zoe* is the life that never ends. *Zoe* is the life God has. *Zoe* is the life God lives. And *Zoe*-life is the life Jesus gives us before we go to the grave.

Indeed Lazarus was not dead. His *bios* was gone, sure...but he was not truly dead because he had *zoe*. He was alive.

Then Jesus asked Martha a question, "Martha, do you believe this?" Martha believed, and Jesus actually brought Lazarus back to earth to spend some more time with his family. That was Jesus' gift to Mary and Martha, but probably not to Lazarus. Poor Lazarus—who would want to come back to earth after being in heaven, only to experience physical death again?

But that is not the important part of this story. The significance here is that we can have the zoe life because of what Jesus has done for us. Lazarus had believed in Jesus. Lazarus had, therefore, begun to live in Jesus. When Lazarus "died," he did not really die in the ultimate sense. Only his bios died.

CLOSING

We have two options concerning the question of life. We can live our lives based on what we have done with our lives—the bios that someday will die. Or we can live our lives based on what Jesus has done with his life—the zoe that lives forever. Lazarus took the second option. So have I. So have many of you. Because of what Jesus did with his life, death does not have the last word. It only has the second-to-last word—which might seem impressive, but it still makes death a great, big loser!

How you answer the question, "How do you plan to escape death?" depends on which kind of life you choose—bios life or zoe life. Your bios, your physical life given to you by your parents, will die. But your zoe will never die.

Would you like to have that life? Pray with me right now.

Let's pray.

SMALL GROUP QUESTIONS

1. **Around the Circle:** What is the best entertainment event you have ever experienced (a concert, a play, a movie, a magician, etc.)?

2. **Ask Just a Few:** Why are so many people afraid of death?

3. **Ask Just a Few:** What are the two Greek words used in the New Testament that are each translated into the word "life"? What do they each mean? (*Bios* is the life we receive from our parents; *zoe* is the life that never ends.)

4. **Ask Just a Few:** When we die here on earth, which life ends? (*Bios*)

In the Bible passage we just heard, Jesus' good friend Lazarus just died. But Jesus offered hope to his sisters:

[23]Jesus said to her, "Your brother will rise again."

[24]Martha answered, "I know he will rise again in the resurrection at the last day."

[25]Jesus said to her, "I am the resurrection and the life. The one who believes in me will live, even though they die; [26]and whoever lives by believing in me will never die. Do you believe this?"

(John 11:23-26)

5. **Ask Just a Few:** When Jesus told Martha, "The one who believes in me will live, even though they die"...which word for *life* was he talking about? (Leader—answer you may be looking for: He who believes in Jesus will zoe, even though his bios will die.)

6. **Ask Just a Few:** According to verse 25, how does a person get this zoe—this life that never ends?

7. **Around the Circle:** Jesus asked Martha, "Do you believe this?" What would you say if Jesus asked you that question to your face tonight?

8. **Around the Circle:** Forgiveness is free to anyone willing to put his or her trust in Jesus. Would any of you like to receive that forgiveness right now? (Take the pressure off interested parties by suggesting the group members close their eyes and raise their hands if they're interested in receiving Christ.)

TALK 21
TITLE: JACKSON'S HOLE

TOPICS: Stuff, Temporary Versus Eternal

BIG IDEA: The momentary troubles and discomforts of this life are but a blip on the radar of eternity.

SCRIPTURE

> [17]For our light and momentary troubles are achieving for us an eternal glory that far outweighs them all. [18]So we fix our eyes not on what is seen, but on what is unseen, since what is seen is temporary, but what is unseen is eternal. (2 Corinthians 4:17-18)

PARTICULARS

When you tell this story, the immediate reaction is, "How could anyone be so stupid?" Just as the biblical storytellers, such as Nathan and Jesus, used such a far-fetched story to make their point, you can use this story to make the point that "the momentary troubles and discomforts of this life are but a blip on the radar of eternity."

I included lots of fun details to the story. Feel free to omit and make the story fit your storytelling style. You'll find that some of the details (room number, description of the bedspread) don't matter. They are just descriptive tools I use to paint a picture.

THE STORY

Jackson wasn't a rich man, or a wise man for that matter. But he was good at his job and was described by his peers as focused and determined.

Jackson was a software engineer for a big mobile technology corporation out of Dallas, Texas. His job often put him on the road for a week at a time. This meant spending a week at a hotel...er...motel. You see, Jackson's company was truly "cheap." The company called this "prudent accounting," but it was just "cheap." They only provided $50 a night for lodging, and that often meant that Jackson was forced to stay in motels that "could use a little work."

Jackson was single and made a meager salary. His apartment in Dallas wasn't very plush. He never bought furniture and didn't spend much money on fancy things. But somehow over the last 10 years Jackson had managed to put away about $9,000 in savings. Jackson never touched this account. His savings account was sacred.

One Sunday afternoon Jackson hopped on a plane from DFW to the Ontario airport in southern California, a short drive to his destination in Bakersfield.

If you've ever been to California, you probably skipped Bakersfield—it's hot, far from the ocean, and...well let's just say that it's not Huntington Beach!

When Jackson landed, he popped into his economy rental car and drove to the motel he reserved, a small chain known as the Super 7 (not quite as popular as its sister chain of greater numerical value). The lady at the counter was cordial, taking an imprint of his credit card and handing him his room key—an actual key, not one of those cool key cards like most other reputable chains had.

"Room 108. Last room," she chirped. "Good thing you had the reservation."

"Yes," Jackson said, raising his eyebrows. "Good thing."

Jackson walked back outside and pulled his car around to the parking spot near room 108. He gathered his things and made his way to the door, fumbling for the room key. As he turned the key and entered the room, he paused to take in the meager surroundings.

Jackson had stayed at some real dives before. But this room took the cake. The wallpaper was peeling in the corner, the industrial carpet was stained, and the stitching was frayed and torn on the cheap '70s bedspread. His eyes wandered over to the small wood desk in the corner of the room. The surface was water stained and chipped. The wobbly little chair didn't match.

Jackson sighed and plopped his bag on the bed. The springs squeaked, groaning under the weight of Jackson's light little carry-on.

It would have to do.

Monday wasn't a great day. The client Jackson was supposed to assist was impossible to please. Each task Jackson embarked on took three times the time projected. The hour hand on the clock quickly found itself past 7 p.m., and Jackson decided that he'd have to tap out and try again the next day.

Jackson hit the drive-thru on the way back to the motel, spending the paltry amount of cash he had remaining from the day's food per diem. With a to-go bag resting in the front seat, he pulled into the familiar oil-stained spot in front of room 108.

"Home sweet home," Jackson muttered to himself, gathering his things.

As Jackson entered the dreary room once again, he set the bag of fast-food cuisine on the desk and meandered over to the TV to turn on the game. Jackson had worked late the night before, prepping for his day with the client, so he never even touched the TV. It was a small 25" with no remote and a smattering of fingerprints on the screen.

He pressed the POWER button with his forefinger.

Nothing.

"You've got to be kidding me!" he snarled.

Jackson checked the cord. Sure enough, it was plugged in. A nearby lamp was plugged in to the same outlet. Jackson clicked the switch, turning it on and sending three moths scurrying to the ceiling.

"Nice," Jackson mumbled under his breath.

After a few more tries, Jackson picked up the phone, read the faded instruction card, and dialed "7" for the front desk.

The phone rang just once, and a high-pitched voice answered. "Super 7 with super service. How can I help you?"

"Yeah, this is Mr. Fife in room 108. Your TV isn't working so..." Jackson thought about his wording. "...so super. Actually...it's not working at all."

"Awww, I'm awfully sorry," Super-Lady cooed. "I'll make a note for the manager to get it fixed next week."

"Next week?" Jackson moaned. "What do you mean next week?"

"The manager doesn't get back until next week, and he's the one that calls Hank to come out and do all the TV repairs."

"Hank?"

"Yes. Hank Shade. He's the owner/operator of Hanks."

Jackson was thoroughly confused. "Hanks?"

"Yes Hanks. Hanks is the electronic shop we use. The one on Riley?" she posed as a question, almost as if Jackson should know where that is. "He services all our TVs and replaces them when they need replacing. Bud will call him next week."

Jackson thought for a second: Bud's the manager. He was starting to figure out Super-Lady's navigation of thought.

"Yes."

Jackson's mind wandered as he attempted to take this all in. No TV for the entire week, the one escape he had looked forward to all day. Gone.

Jackson switched ears so he could reach his left hand out and shoo two flies away from his dinner. The voice on the phone broke the awkward silence.

"Anything else I can do for you?"

"No. Everything's just super!" Jackson hung up, plopped in the wobbly chair, shooed another fly and began to eat his cold French fries.

A moment later Jackson stopped mid-chew with an epiphany.

He picked up the phone and dialed 411. "What's the number for Hanks on Riley?"

Seconds later he was dialing Hanks. It rang three times and then a man picked up. "Hanks, this is Hank."

"Hank!" Jackson said, as if they were old friends. "I'm calling from the Super 7 over here. Bud mentioned you were the one to call."

There was silence on the other line. Jackson was just about to repeat the sentence when Hank spoke. "I thought Bud was in Vegas."

"Yes," Jackson rejoined. "For the next week. But we've got a problem with the TV in room 108 right now. Can't wait for Bud."

The voice on the other end was uncomfortably silent once again.

Jackson began to second-guess his pathetic little plan. Hank was onto him. Jackson was sure of it. He thought about just hanging up, but Hank spoke. "Okay, I'll be right over."

Jackson stared at the receiver as he hung it up.

"Yeah!" he cheered to himself. He couldn't believe what just happened. It worked.

Twenty minutes later there was a knock at the door. Jackson opened it to see a middle-aged man with thick eyebrows leaning on the doorframe and holding a small red toolbox.

"Hank?" Jackson asked.

"Always has been. Probably will be for a few years more, too," he quipped.

Jackson feigned a smile. "Well, come in. Come in!"

Hank tinkered with the TV for only a few minutes before turning to Jackson. "It's DOA."

"What's that mean?" Jackson asked, glancing at his watch, wondering if the game was in the fourth quarter by now.

"Means this thing was dead when I got here and its condition ain't gonna change. Need a new TV, that's all."

"Great," Jackson said hopefully. "Did you bring one?"

Hank stopped collecting his tools and looked up at Jackson skeptically. "Well, no. Not for here. Gotta wait for Bud to tell me what he wants. And Bud is..."

"...in Vegas," Jackson said, finishing Hank's sentence. "I know. For a week. But this room needs a TV now. Come on. You know Bud's gonna replace it."

"I don't even have the right TV. I only have a 50-inch plasma in the van. That's for a home delivery I've got tomorrow. Actually got two of 'em. Panasonics. Great TVs." He chuckled and talked through the side of his mouth. "Much better than Bud will ever put in here."

Something in Jackson's head snapped. "I'll take one." Jackson almost couldn't believe the words as they left his mouth.

Hank just stared at Jackson, wiping his hands on a small orange rag from his toolbox. "Can't do it."

Jackson's smile disappeared. "What do you mean you can't do it? I'll pay for it. Right now." Jackson pulled out his wallet.

Hank shook his head and waved his palm at Jackson. "I...I can't do that. Bud's a long-time customer. He bought every one of these 87 TV sets from me and calls me every time he needs a new one. I can't go and put a personal TV in a room for someone, that's a conflict of interest. If I were..."

"That's not a conflict of interest," Jackson interrupted. "Bud's TV doesn't work! This is a special situation. Come on!" Jackson held out his credit card.

Hank shook his head back and forth. "Can't do it. I only install TVs that I can bolt down here at the Super 7."

Jackson pondered Hank's words, reflecting on his horrible day.

He cursed the thought of his cheap boss, this cheap motel, his high-maintenance client. He looked around the room at his bleak, miserable surroundings. The bedspread looked like puke. The desk was something from World War II. The carpet smelled like soiled diaper. And now...no TV!

Jackson wasn't about to turn back now. "Then bolt it down!"

Hank scratched his head. "What are you saying, boy?"

"Bolt it down. I'll buy that TV for the Super 7. Just make sure it works and have it on before the game is over, and you've got a sale."

Hank looked back and forth as if to check that no one else was listening in. "So you're gonna personally buy a 50" plasma from me for the Super 7 just so you can watch it for one week?" Hank asked, wrinkling his nose.

Jackson had never been so sure of something his entire life. "Yep. And a Blu-ray player, too!"

About 45 minutes later Hank turned on the newly installed plasma and tuned it in to the last six minutes of the game. Jackson watched until the clock ran out while Hank cleaned up the boxes and carried the old motel TV back to the truck. Hank even waited for the commercials before drilling and bolting the plasma's feet to the entertainment center, which was probably the only piece of furniture that didn't need replacing in the entire room.

After paying Hank and signing several papers disclosing that the TV was the property of the Super 7, Jackson shut the door and plopped on the bed to enjoy the new 50" screen. As his body hit the bed, the springs groaned once again.

Jackson thought for a moment...and picked up the phone. "Get me the closest store that sells mattresses!"

The next day went by incredibly quickly for Jackson. The client was just as bad as the day before, but Jackson didn't care. He glanced at his watch. Almost 4 p.m.

"I'm outta here," Jackson declared.

"What?" the client asked, thoroughly confused.

"Bed's being delivered at 4:30, and I have to pay the painters."

Jackson didn't even wait for a response. He headed to his new rental car, a convertible Mustang he traded in during lunch for the compact he began his week with.

Seven minutes later he pulled up in front of room 108 right next to the painters' van. When Jackson walked in the room he barely recognized the place. The carpet installers had finished at noon. It was a good thing they took his credit card over the phone. They charged an extra $200 to do it on such short notice. The painters had torn off the wallpaper and painted the room in a nice twotone: "Red brawn" and "Snip of Tannin." He let the girl on the phone from the paint store choose because he figured she knew better. They were finishing up the trim when the furniture arrived. Luckily the bedding store had desks, dressers and even a comfy recliner.

The next evening Jackson kicked back in his recliner eating Chinese food watching the newest *Avengers* film on Blu-ray. The surround sound was amazing. Those wireless speakers he had installed in each corner of the room really delivered. It was almost like he could hear Ironman flying around behind him.

The days went by quickly that week, and the evenings were sheer paradise for Jackson, something he had never experienced.

Then Friday came. As he turned in the room key that morning...it hit him. The truth he knew all along...but hadn't dealt with until now. The temporary comforts of the room were a thing of the past!

Friday dragged on painfully. He escaped the client's office at 3 p.m. to make his evening flight. When he took his seat on the plane, it wouldn't recline. It was broken.

Late that night, back at his own apartment, Jackson logged on to his credit card's site.

Recent charges: $8,742.82

He transferred the $9,000 from his savings. He had $257 and change left over.

As Jackson leaned back in his chair, he looked around his apartment. The couch was torn in the front. His TV was puny and old. His carpet was tattered and stained.

If only... he thought.

Exactly 1,448 miles to the west, a hotel manager named Bud kicked up his feet on the new recliner in room 108 watching a movie on Blu-ray. He tossed a handful of popcorn in his mouth and sighed, "I love my job."

TRANSITION STATEMENT

What kind of idiot would spend all of their savings for a few days of pleasure? Jackson must have blown a gasket. As the week went on, his spending binge became more out of control.

APPLICATION AND SCRIPTURE

The storytellers in Scripture would often use a story about such a fool to get the listeners to see themselves. Nathan used the story of a person who stole another man's pet lamb to get David to see that he stole another man's wife. Jesus used a similar style of story to get his listeners to see their own hypocrisy. He often ended his stories with a penetrating question.

The story of Jackson's motel room binge serves the same purpose.

Often we can't see that in many ways we are just like Jackson, living for a quick, temporary thrill with no regard for the future. In what ways are we just like Jackson when we consider the eternal kingdom of God?

The Christian lives in two worlds: our temporary life on earth, and our eternal life living for the kingdom. Some people misunderstand the concept of "God's kingdom." God's kingdom isn't just some place where we go when we die. God's kingdom is active here and now, and those of us who put our trust in Jesus can start experiencing the joy of kingdom-living right now.

The question you need to consider is: Which world are you living for?

The writers of Scripture knew that one of the great temptations for Christians is that we would want to neglect the eternal kingdom in order to live as comfortably as possible in this temporary dwelling place—the present earth. Therefore, Jesus told his disciples:

But seek first his kingdom and his righteousness, and all these things will be given to you as well. (Matthew 6:33)

The Apostle Paul also talked about living in these two worlds when he said in 2 Corinthians 4:17-18:

[17]For our light and momentary troubles are achieving for us an eternal glory that far outweighs them all. [18]So we fix our eyes not on what is seen, but on what is unseen, since what is seen is temporary, but what is unseen is eternal.

Jackson's momentary troubles, or shall we call it *discomfort*, were only going to last for four nights. And when you compare that to the rest of his life...that's tiny.

Paul is saying that the "momentary troubles" of this present time are but a blip on the radar of eternity.

As difficult as it is to spend four nights in a cheap motel with no TV, it pales in comparison to eternal life with God. Why would anyone abuse their life savings for four measly nights?

Why would anyone mess with his or her eternal soul for temporary earthly pleasures?

Paul offers us some comfort here and now by giving us a glimpse at the big picture. Notice how Paul says that the glory outweighs the grief— "outweighs" being the key word. If you had a pair of cosmic scales, and you put all of your discomforts on one side and all of the joys and the new heaven and new earth that God has promised to us on the other, our grief would seem so insignificant—and yet we keep putting all of our resources into trying to make us comfortable in this life that we neglect God's eternal kingdom which lasts forever.

Stuff is fun. Stuff can be wonderful. Stuff can be good...unless it becomes what we seek.

Stuff is just temporary. But God's kingdom lasts forever.

CLOSING

I'll be honest. I love stuff. I love the smell of a new car, the feel of new clothes, and the sound of new speakers. And nothing is wrong with this... unless stuff becomes such a distraction that I try to use it to satisfy my short life on this earth instead of pursuing God's eternal kingdom.

Which world are you living for?

Paul reminds us that our stuff will soon be gone, but the kingdom of God will last forever. When I forget this reality...I become as stupid and shortsighted as Jackson.

SMALL GROUP QUESTIONS

1. **Around the Circle:** If you could stay at any hotel anywhere in the world, where would you stay?

2. **Ask Just a Few:** Why do you think Jackson spent his life savings on a motel room only for a week?

3. **Ask Just a Few:** Why is this stupid?

The Christian lives in two worlds: our temporary life on earth, and our eternal life living for the kingdom. The Apostle Paul talked about living in these two worlds when he said in 2 Corinthians 4:17-18:

17For our light and momentary troubles are achieving for us an eternal glory that far outweighs them all. 18So we fix our eyes not on what is seen, but on what is unseen, since what is seen is temporary, but what is unseen is eternal.

4. **Ask Just a Few:** What does Paul call our current troubles?

5. **Ask Just a Few:** Why does he describe them this way?

6. **Ask Just a Few:** What advice, in verse 18, does he give us? How does this advice help remind us that our "momentary troubles" are just a blip on the radar of eternity?

7. **Ask Just a Few:** What are some ways we can "fix our eyes" on "what is unseen"?

8. **Around the Circle:** Which world are you living for? Is that smart...or is that just as shortsighted as Jackson?

9. **Around the Circle:** Forgiveness is free to anyone willing to put his or her trust in Jesus. Would any of you like to receive that forgiveness right now? (Take the pressure off interested parties by suggesting the group members close their eyes and raise their hands if they're interested in receiving Christ.)

TALK 22

TITLE: UNBROKEN

TOPICS: New Life, Forgiveness, Freedom from Bitterness

BIG IDEA: No matter who has tried to break and humiliate us, through Christ we can be made new people of strength, love, and forgiveness.

SCRIPTURE

> Therefore, if anyone is in Christ, he is a new creation; the old has gone, the new has come!
> (2 Corinthians 5:17, NIV 1984)

PARTICULARS

This is the true story of the life transformation of Louis Zamperini. He was a juvenile delinquent, Olympic track star, survivor of 47 days on a life raft, and a POW full of anger and hatred. But Christ changed him and he became a totally new person. At this writing (2012) Louis is 94 and still going strong, speaking and telling his story. The particulars of this account are from two sources, his speeches and the best-selling book, *Unbroken*, by Laura Hillenbrand. There are several quotes in the story. I would suggest you copy them down and put them on a small card to read at the appropriate time in the story, or you could memorize them.

STORY

Louis Zamperini was a juvenile delinquent turned Olympic track star who ran in the 1936 Olympics. His running career started in grade school—running from the cops. He was always in trouble.

Louis' life had many defining moments. One of the first ones was when his brother, who never gave up on Louis, got the police chief to bring him to the police station to show him two guys in the lockup. He said, "Louis, those two guys have lost the most precious thing in life: freedom. Someday you're going to end up behind bars." The police chief suggested that Louis get into running, after all, they had been chasing him all over town for months.

Louis must have listened, because he started running for his high school. Fact of the matter, Louis was the only runner from his school. Louis recalls one of his early races when he was coming down the home stretch in fourth place. He heard the students from his school screaming from the grandstand, "Come on, Louis!" Louis was amazed. He had no idea anybody knew his name. With a newfound confidence, he poured on speed, passed one guy and came in third.

This was a pivotal moment in his life. Louis decided that he had enough of getting in trouble and instead would dedicate himself to becoming a runner. He became fanatical about training. He started winning races, and he never lost a mile race for five years.

On the strength of his running, he was invited to New York for the 1936 Olympic trials and made the team on the 5,000 meter run. But Louis lost sight of his goal while on the 12-day boat ride to Europe and gained 15 pounds. Realizing what he'd done, he tried to lose it when he arrived in Berlin, just a few days before the finals, but he couldn't shed it all. He was in great shape, but the extra weight kept him from keeping up with the fast pace that the Finns set. On the last lap there were seven runners ahead of him. He was 50 yards behind. As he looked at the runners ahead of him he remembered what his brother, his coach, had told him. "Everybody is tired the last lap," his brother would say. "Think of it this way. Isn't one minute of pain worth a lifetime of glory? So just go out and run your guts out."

Energized by those thoughts, Louis sprinted the last lap, and as he gained the 50 yards on the leaders, the crowd went wild, standing and cheering him on. He never passed the seven runners, coming in eighth; but his sprint became legendary as he ran the last lap of the 5,000 meters in only 56 seconds.

Hitler even sent an officer over to Louis with this message: "Hitler wants to see you." Louis said that Hitler took his hand and said, "The boy with the fast finish." That was it.

His brother was right. One minute of pain was a lifetime of glory, and people were still talking about that last lap.

Louis still had a little bit of the old Louis in him. While at the Olympics, he climbed a flagpole and stole the personal flag of Hitler. But his ornery spirit didn't distract him from his running. Two years later in 1938 as co-captain of the USC track squad, Zamperini set a national collegiate mile record (4:08.3) which held for 15 years.

When World War II broke out Louis joined the Army Air Force (that's what the Air Force was called back then) and was commissioned as second lieutenant. During his service, Louis was on a flight over the ocean and his plane crashed. Only three members of the crew survived the crash: Louis, the pilot Phil and a tail gunner, Mac. The three of them spent 47 days on a raft.

One day a Japanese plane used them for target practice for more than 30 minutes, making 48 holes in the raft. Louis would dive into the water and hide under the raft to avoid getting hit by the bullets, all while keeping his eye out for sharks. One of their greatest threats during those

47 days was sharks, as every day the sharks kept bumping their raft. On one occasion a great white shark actually leaped into the raft. Louis punched the shark in the nose with both of his palms and recounted, "I was able to shove the ravenous creature back into the sea."

Sharks and Japanese planes aside, the major problems on the raft were water and food. At the very beginning of their time on the life raft, while Phil and Louis were asleep, Mac ate all of the food that they had grabbed from the plane. So the small group was forced to live on what they caught from the ocean.

The first time an albatross landed in their raft, they caught it and used it for fishing bait because it tasted so bitter. But by the third time it happened, they were so hungry that they just ate the large seabird. Louis said, "We ate the entire bird with gusto. This time it tasted like a hot fudge sundae. I ate the eyeballs and all the rest." Louis lost more than 100 pounds and weighed only 66 pounds when he got off the raft.

Although there were the terrible experiences of hallucinations and shark attacks, Louis experienced times when everything was still and beautiful. The water was so smooth it was like a mirror. He remembered a little minnow that jumped out of the water about 50 yards away, and they could hear it. There were moments like that when they had beautiful sunrises, sunsets. It was at times like these that Louis thought, *There is a God*. Other times when Louis was in deep suffering and pain, he even cried, praying, making promises that he would devote his life to God if he could get home alive. These were promises that he would forget for quite some time.

On the 47th day the three men saw an island and became hopeful, but as they were making their way there, a Japanese patrol boat spotted them and picked them up. Life was about to become a living nightmare.

The three captives ultimately were taken to Execution Island. Louis ended up on that island for 43 unbearable days in a small cell about 28 inches wide, buzzing with flies and disease-carrying mosquitoes. Louis didn't know what would be better, another day in the confined chamber or execution. Louis was confident that execution would come.

On execution day a Japanese officer from another division on the island recognized Louis. This particular officer followed the Olympics and American sports and knew all about Louis. He suggested to the panel that rather than executing him, they should send him to Tokyo to make radio propaganda broadcasts. Consequently, Louis was sent to a private interrogation camp to read the script written for him.

But when he read what they wanted him to say, he refused. (Louis actually stole the script, and it is published in his book.) Because he refused, he was sent to a punishment camp that would prove the darkest moments of his POW experience.

It was at this POW camp that Louis met the man who would make his life miserable for the next two years. This guard was nicknamed "the Bird." The Bird hated Louis and wanted to make an example of the annoyingly optimistic Olympic runner. For two years, the Bird tried to break Louis' spirit with physical and emotional torture. When Louis lay unconscious on the floor after a beating, the Bird would pick him up and offer him some sort of kindness...only to knock down again.

Zamperini's torture began transcending the physical during his last year in prison. Soon Louis' worst enemies were his own nightmares. Louis started having dreams of strangling the Bird, nightmares that continued after the war was over and Louis returned home. The anger, hatred, and bitterness that gestated within Louis were slowly decaying his life away.

Still, he was invited to parties and was welcomed home by his many friends and family. He soon met and married the girl of his dreams. Life seemed great for Louis. Mostly. After all, he was home.

But Louis' nightmares increased. One night Louis dreamed he was strangling the Bird. When he woke up his hands were around his wife's throat. Zamperini was dealing with post-traumatic stress disorder, but no one knew what it was back then.

Louis began drowning his pain with alcohol, attempting to escape from the anger and nightmares. His wife was so scared that she thought the only answer was to leave Louis, so she filed for divorce.

As both of their lives unraveled, a young evangelist by the name of Billy Graham came to L.A., speaking at one of his first crusades. Some friends invited Louis and his wife to attend. Louis refused, but his wife went to the meeting. She came back excited because she found peace and joy in her heart when she received Christ as her savior. She kept inviting Louis to the meetings, but he wanted no part of that. He kept refusing until one day she told him, "Because of my conversion, I'm not getting a divorce."

He loved his wife and was so thrilled that she decided to stay with him that he agreed to attend the Graham crusade. But during the sermon Louis grabbed his wife and said, "We're out of here" and pulled her home. He swore he would never go back. But when she reminded Louis that she wasn't going to get a divorce because of her conversion, he went back. Near the end of Graham's sermon, the evangelist mentioned that when people come to the end of their ropes and there's nowhere else to turn, they turn to God.

Louis knew that was where he was, so he surrendered to God. Louis immediately experienced four miracles.

The first miracle happened the night when he gave his life to Christ. He went back to the prayer room and made a confession of his faith in Christ. As the message of Christ's love and forgiveness was explained to Louis, he got on his knees and prayed. Before he ever realized what was happening, Louis prayed and forgave all the guards that held him captive...even the Bird. It was a miracle.

The second genuine miracle happened that next morning. He got up and grabbed a New Testament that was given to him in the Army Air Force. Many of the men had never read it in the service because they didn't understand it, so they threw them in their footlockers and forgot about them. But that morning he went to a park bench and started to read. He understood what he was reading. It was a miracle.

The third miracle was his freedom from alcohol. The first thing Louis did was pour all the alcohol in his home down the drain. He was done drinking.

The fourth miracle was when he woke up, it was the first night he had not had a nightmare about the Bird—and he would never have another nightmare. Louis said, "It's as if the doctor had cut the hating part of my brain away."

TRANSITION STATEMENT

Laura Hillenbrand writes about Zamperini in her best-selling book about his life, *Unbroken*: "He was not the worthless, broken, forsaken man that the Bird had striven to make of him. In a single silent moment his rage, fear, humiliation, and helplessness had fallen away. That morning he believed he was a new creation."

APPLICATION AND SCRIPTURE

No matter who has tried to break and humiliate us, through Christ we can be made new people of strength, love, and forgiveness.

Louis was a new person. His life was changed. The Bible describes this transformation in 2 Corinthians 5:17:

Therefore, if anyone is in Christ, he is a new creation; the old has gone, the new has come! (NIV 1984)

The Apostle Paul is writing about his own life. He had been transformed from a self-righteous, religious fanatic who depended on his own works and power to a whole new person. Paul was responsible for killing Christians in his effort to stop this new movement called Christianity. He hated Christ. Yet after his conversion, he would go on to write most of the New Testament and start churches all over the European and Asian continents.

Similarly, God transformed Louis from an angry and tormented man to a new person. For Louis that transformation began immediately. Not everyone can report that kind of miracle, but everyone can report that when they accept God's forgiveness through Christ, he begins the work of a new creation.

Louis became a professional speaker, speaking all over the world to millions of people about the topic of forgiveness. He loved to share his story about how God turned his life of hatred, anger, drunkenness, and nightmares into a life of love and forgiveness through Jesus Christ. He demonstrated his new life by starting a boy's camp and working with the homeless.

CLOSING

Some of you in this place feel the weight of your hatred, your anger, and your nightmares because of what you have experienced in this life. You may have been rejected by the people you depended on for love. Some of you have been sexually assaulted, mistreated, abused emotionally and physically. Some of you are being mistreated at school, home, or work. And like Louis, you perhaps make promises to God that if he would only get you out...but that time hasn't come to you yet.

Today is the day to pray to God for his love and forgiveness. Through the cross of Jesus Christ, where he was abused, mistreated, mocked and killed, and you have the forgiveness for our sins and forgiveness from the most terrible thing that we have ever experienced.

God loves you and wants to heal you from your pain and brokenness.

Let's pray.

SMALL GROUP QUESTIONS

1. **Around the Circle:** What is your favorite place to go for fun?

2. **Ask Just a Few:** What negative behaviors did Louis begin once he was free from the POW camp?

3. **Ask Just a Few:** How did his drinking and bitterness affect his marriage?

4. **Ask Just a Few:** What saved Louis from alcohol, divorce, and his nightmares?

Louis went to hear Billy Graham speak about Jesus, and Louis became a completely new person with Christ now in his heart. His life was changed. The Bible describes this transformation in 2 Corinthians 5:17:

Therefore, if anyone is in Christ, he is a new creation; the old has gone, the new has come! (NIV 1984)

5. **Ask Just a Few:** What does living "in Christ" mean?

6. **Ask Just a Few:** According to the verse, what happens if you put your trust "in Christ"? (You become a new creation.)

7. **Ask Just a Few:** What happens to the old stuff in your life? What could be some of that stuff?

8. **Around the Circle:** What might your life look like if you became a new creation?

9. **Around the Circle:** Would you like to experience the new life that Louis experienced? Forgiveness is free to anyone willing to put his or her trust in Jesus. Would any of you like to receive that forgiveness right now? (Take the pressure off interested parties by suggesting the group members close their eyes and raise their hands if they're interested in receiving Christ.)

TALK 23
TITLE: LET GO

TOPICS: True Faith, Surrendering to God

BIG IDEA: Saving faith is more than intellectual information or emotional feelings about God; it is totally trusting God with your actions.

SCRIPTURE

> You believe that there is one God. Good! Even the demons believe that—and shudder. (James 2:19)

PARTICULARS

This fictional story is based on a true story that happened to someone very close to me. I've told the real story numerous times when presenting the gospel, and young people really connect with the analogy of what it means to truly trust, not just through words, but through actions.

STORY

As 12-year-old Nicole gripped the rock wall with her hands alone, she didn't dare look down. When her rubber shoes slipped from their foothold she knew she was in trouble, and she didn't know how long she could keep her grip.

Ralston Peak was no beginner's climb. After a seven-mile hike gaining more than 2,000 feet in elevation, the face of the peak extended vertically more than 100 feet straight up, with rocks at the base. Nicki was dangling more than 80 feet from the jagged rocks below. No one could survive that fall.

She thought of her daddy's words: "You don't need to impress your brother and sister Nicki. Safety over pride."

In hindsight, she regretted not listening to her dad's advice. In the moment, she didn't feel like a free solo climber anymore. She was just a little girl hanging on for her life, wishing her daddy were there to save her.

Nicki's family loved free climbing. Nicki's dad was old school and preferred traditional free climbing with multiple climbers, where the leader places cams and attaches the rope with the bottom climber belaying. This way, if the top climber falls, he or she usually only fell a few meters before the safety of the harness took hold.

Nicki had experienced several falls like that, and while grateful for the harness, they were never pleasant experiences. The feeling of free falling for even a second was terrifying, and the sudden jerk of the harness wrenched your entire body.

Jeff and Sarah, Nicki's older brother and sister, preferred free soloing. This is where climbers use no ropes, no harness...nothing but a chalk bag, a good pair of shoes, and strong hands. Jeff and Sarah hadn't climbed anything higher than 100 feet, but anything over 20 is technically free soloing. That's what they were doing on this particular day; and Nicki was trying to keep up.

Nicki was an experienced climber. Her dad taught her to free climb when she was seven. Nicki always felt safe with her dad around. His rule was "safety first." He taught her how to check a harness, inspect a rope, and how to hook up to cams or preplaced hangers. "Hangers are the arms that catch you if I'm not here to catch your fall," her dad would always say.

But Nicki was competitive and often felt the pressure to try to keep up with her brother and sister. They didn't push her to try to climb beyond her ability. Jeff and Sarah just loved climbing without rope and harness. Nicki, wanting to be with them, usually followed.

Nicki's first free solo was at a popular jumping rock at the American River not three miles from her house. The rock was a tall vertical face that extended about 60 feet up from the river below. Teenagers would jump off the top of the cliff to the river below. Nicki and her siblings had no interest in cliff diving. Instead, they would start at the bottom, climbing out of the water and up the face. If they slipped...no big deal. They just fell back into the water below. It was the perfect free solo practice ground.

Nicki's next climb was at an indoor climbing place called Granite Walls. It attracted crowds ranging from birthday party guests to experienced climbers. All climbing at Granite Walls was with ropes and harnesses. That's why Nicki got kicked out.

The largest wall there was called the North Face. It was more than 45 feet tall and was very difficult. Her sister Sarah made a wisecrack to Nicki about not being able to do it—with a harness. Nicki jumped on the wall and scaled it in less than five minutes with no harness, beating her sister's record by over a minute. Four employees were waiting for her when she reached the bottom, and Nicki was escorted out of the building with a very clear, "You're not welcome back."

Nicki, Jeff, and Sarah had done several climbs since Granite Walls. Nicki was obviously very skilled. Maybe even more than Sarah, despite the fact that Nikki was five years younger.

When the family camped next to Ralston Peak, the huge cliff face beckoned them, daring them to climb. Nicki's dad told them, "Tomorrow we'll free climb it. Rest up. In the meantime, don't go getting so eager that you get stupid."

Jeff was probably the one to blame for attempting the climb free solo not an hour after his dad warned him not to. He said he just wanted to warm up a little. Sarah was quick to follow, possibly trying to prove that she was just as good. Nicki followed just a few minutes later.

What might have started as just a warm-up became the largest free solo climb the kids had ever attempted. Before they knew it, Jeff and Sarah had both ascended over 50 feet, and there was no turning around at this point. When Jeff hit 65 feet he found a small ledge about 2 feet wide where he was able to stop and rest. The face only extended about another 40 feet from there. As soon as Sarah and Nicki made it to the ledge, Jeff started up the remaining 40 feet. A minute later, Sarah followed, with Nicki at her heels.

The next 10 feet were probably the hardest of the entire climb. The face jutted out a couple feet, like a ceiling, forcing the climber to reach back and hold his or her body upside down for a moment. Granite Walls had several practice walls with these kinds of obstacles. The kids had conquered them dozens of times. But today it was at this impasse that Nicki lost her footing. She had been so focused on trying to keep up with Jeff and Sarah that she didn't find a secure foothold. As her foot slipped, her hands instinctively grabbed tightly, but it was only a matter of seconds before her body swung out and she dangled free, hanging on only with her hands.

Nicki was normally able to lift her own body weight and negotiate another handhold. But panic had set in. Nicki had never been this high up with no harness. Plus, she had been overextending herself already. Her grip and her forearms were fatigued and groaned in pain. It was no use. She was stuck.

Her heart began racing, her breathing quickened, and tears started to flow from her eyes. This was it. She was sure that there was no way getting out of this one.

And that's when she heard the familiar voice 10 feet below her.

"Nicki, relax."

She knew the voice well but didn't have time for explanation. "Daddy! I can't hold on."

"You're doing fine Nicki. Just hold fast for another few seconds."

Nicki heard the familiar sound of her dad anchoring a cam to a crack in the rock below and the click of a carabiner.

Nicki was atop an emotional roller coaster. Survival trumped everything right now, but knowing that this might be her last conversation with her dad, she was compelled to set things right.

"I'm so sorry, Daddy!" she quickly blurted out. "So sorry!"

"Don't worry about that now, Nicki. Let's just get you down."

"But I can't hold on. My fingers are slipping," Nicki said frantically. She felt her grip weakening. She knew she couldn't hold on much longer.

And that's when her dad said something unanticipated. "Nicki, do you trust me?"

"What?" Nicki asked, surprised.

"No time for discussion, Nicki," her dad replied. "Do you trust me?"

Nicki's mind flashed with all the times her dad was there for her. He taught her everything there was to know about climbing. He taught her how to tie in, how to belay, even how to fall. Whenever Nicki fell, her daddy was always there to pick her up. But how could he possibly save her this time? Nicki didn't know and didn't care. She trusted him.

"Yes, I trust you. Help me."

Nicki's dad paused for just a second; then he spoke with confidence and certainty.

"Then let go."

Nicki's dad was standing on the two-foot ledge that Nicki and her siblings had rested on just moments before. Nicki was dangling only a few feet out of her father's reach. He had quickly secured a cam into a crack and tied on with his harness. He stood with his hands free directly below Nicki.

He repeated himself. "Nicki, I've got you. Let go."

Nicki let go, and she fell into her daddy's arms.

Nicki burst into tears, burying her head into his thick chest.

Nicki's dad set her carefully on her feet on the ledge. Wiping her face with her own sleeve, she looked down. "Daddy, how did you get up here?"

Her dad smiled. "I free soloed."

She laughed. "Dad, you never free solo!"

"Only when my little girl is in trouble. When I saw you three morons climbing the face, I just attached my gear real quick and climbed. No time for anything else."

Nicki smiled. "Alex Honnold's got nothing on you!" Honnold is perhaps the most gifted free soloist on the planet. Nicki's brother had a poster of him in his room.

Nicki's dad laughed. "Yeah, right." He handed her a harness. "Now tie in. Free solo is over. We're gonna go get your brother and sister."

An hour later the four of them were on the ground together walking back to the campsite.

Nicki never free soloed again.

TRANSITION STATEMENT

Nicki's dad asked her a simple question, a question that would be easy to answer in word, but very hard to carry out in action. He asked her, "Nicki, do you trust me?"

Nicki answered, "Yes, I trust you. Help me."

And that's where her father gave her the opportunity to prove her trust, a response that would, in turn, save her.

He simply said, "Then let go."

APPLICATION AND SCRIPTURE

I'll be the first to tell you, there is nothing any of us can do to make ourselves right before God. We've all sinned and all need a savior (Romans 3:23). That's what's so uniquely amazing about Jesus. Unlike other religions, Jesus doesn't require us to earn our righteousness. He knows we've failed, and he is willing to save us, despite our failure (Romans 5:8). The only thing we need to do is admit that fact and depend on him to save us. That true act of faith is what saves us. Jesus is ready to catch us when we can honestly say, "I can't do it! I need your help!"

It all comes down to faith. That's probably why James spends so much time defining what true faith looks like in his letter to the Jewish Christians of the first century.

You believe that there is one God. Good! Even the demons believe that—and shudder. (James 2:19)

James is contrasting false faith with true faith. In the verses to follow, he reveals how true faith proves itself by its deeds. In essence James is saying that saving faith is more than intellectual information or emotional feelings about God; it means totally trusting God with your actions.

The first type of faith that James exposes is intellectual faith. That kind of faith says, "Oh, I believe there is a God. I even know a lot about him. I've gone to church, or Sunday school, or the Christian school." That kind of faith might even say the words, "I've accepted Christ as my savior." But for some of you, it was merely an intellectual exercise because you believe it was the right thing to do, or you just wanted to go to heaven someday. But James says to this kind of faith: "Big deal, even the demons believe that there is one God."

The second variety of faith is emotional faith. James says that not only do the demons believe that God exists, but they are emotional about it. They tremble. There is a kind of faith that has an emotional experience. You might be scared when you fathom God's power. You might get sad when you think of someone who died and respond to God emotionally. But when the tears dry and you get a good night's sleep, you're back to life as usual—with you in charge and Jesus on the sidelines.

Real faith goes way beyond intellectual information or emotional feelings about God. In the next verses James gives two examples of real faith. He asks in verse 20, "Do you want evidence that faith without deeds is useless?" Then he reminds them of their Jewish history and the stories of Abraham and Rahab. When these heroes believed, they acted. True saving faith is based on intellectual knowledge, and often it creates emotional feelings, but James says that authentic faith takes that knowledge and emotion about God and then acts upon it.

In the story about Nicki, when she let go she demonstrated true faith. True faith is more than words. When Nicki's dad asked her, "Do you trust me?" it didn't take a lot of faith to respond, "Yes, I trust you"—but letting go took real faith and demonstrated that she truly trusted him. Letting go proved Nicki meant her words—that is saving faith.

A lot of people try to earn their way to heaven. Thankfully God doesn't work that way. This is good news because no one is perfect and all of us would be doomed. So Jesus requires one thing of us: To totally trust in him to save us. This doesn't mean we need to be perfect—we can't be perfect. That's why we need him in the first place.

Nicki's little free solo is a perfect example of this. She disobeyed her father and got herself in a jam that probably would have cost Nicki her life. But her father showed up to save her, only requiring one thing: Complete trust. Nicki, realizing that her way was futile, put her complete trust in her dad, letting go of her imperfect path, and simply falling into his arms.

Belief in God is so much more than just saying the magic words. That's not belief. True trust in Jesus is admitting we need him and falling into his arms.

CLOSING

Where are you right now? Do you believe God intellectually? Do you feel emotional about him? Neither of these are bad things...but neither of these are "faith."

Are you ready to put your trust in him right now? Because that might be his voice calling to you right now asking you, "Do you trust me?"

If you answer, "Yes"…he might just tell you, "Then let go."

Are you ready to let go of what you're holding on to and fall in his arms?

Let's pray.

SMALL GROUP QUESTIONS

1. **Around the Circle:** What are your best memories with your family?

2. **Ask Just a Few:** Why do you think Nicki followed her brother and sister?

3. **Ask Just a Few:** How do you think Nicki felt when she first heard her dad's voice just 10 feet below her?

4. **Ask Just a Few:** What very important question did her dad ask her?

5. **Ask Just a Few:** What does true trust look like?

6. **Ask Just a Few:** How do we know that Nicki truly trusted her dad, and she wasn't just saying it?

A lot of religions use the word *believe*. Unlike other religions, Christianity doesn't require us to earn our righteousness. Jesus knows we've failed, and he is willing to save us despite our failure (Romans 5:8). The only thing we need to do is admit that fact and depend on him to save us. That true act of faith is what saves us. Jesus is ready to catch us when we can honestly say, "I can't do it! I need your help!"

It all comes down to faith. That's probably why James spent so much time defining what true faith looks like in his letter to the Jewish Christians of the first century.

You believe that there is one God. Good! Even the demons believe that— and shudder. (James 2:10)

7. **Ask Just a Few:** According to this verse, is it good enough to believe that there is a God up there in the sky?

God isn't interested in someone just saying the words, "I believe." He wants us to put our trust in him. God wants us to let go and fall into his arms tonight.

8. **Around the Circle:** Are you ready to put your trust in God right now? Forgiveness is free to anyone willing to put his or her trust in Jesus. Would any of you like to receive that forgiveness right now? (Take the pressure off interested parties by suggesting the group members close their eyes and raise their hands if they're interested in receiving Christ.)

TALK 24
TITLE: SPARING FRANCIS

TOPICS: Salvation, Sacrifice

BIG IDEA: Because one man died, we have life.

SCRIPTURE

> ⁶You see, at just the right time, when we were still powerless, Christ died for the ungodly. ⁷Very rarely will anyone die for a righteous person, though for a good person someone might possibly dare to die. ⁸But God demonstrates his own love for us in this: While we were still sinners, Christ died for us.
> (Romans 5:6-8)

PARTICULARS

The story of Maximilian Kolbe is a very moving account of how one 20th-century godly man gave up his life so another could live. I use this story to illustrate the love of God and how Jesus gave his life so that we might live. The story sets up an explanation of Paul's powerful statement in Romans 5 that even though it is rare that a good man will die for another good man, it is really rare for a good man to die for a sinner. This talk goes pretty deep in a short amount of time, unpacking three key words from the Scripture passage.

(My friend David R. Smith helped me put this talk together, using a story from his free online illustration database, ItsLikeThis.org, an amazing resource for stories and illustrations, organized by topic.)

STORY

If there was one thing Maximilian Kolbe knew how to do, it was to deeply impact the lives of those around him.

Kolbe was a hard-working Catholic priest who served thousands of people throughout war-ravaged Europe before and during World War II. While Father Kolbe did his humble work, millions upon millions were being killed as Adolf Hitler and his bloodthirsty henchmen rampaged across Europe and Russia. Those who were lucky enough to escape death were often forced to flee their homes, their businesses, and even their families.

Everywhere he looked, Father Kolbe saw despair and brokenness in the eyes of men, women, and children. No one was exempt from the cruelty of the Nazis.

Not even Kolbe himself.

When the war broke out in September 1939, Kolbe found himself taking care of a flood of Jewish refugees that began making their way into his native Poland. The kind-hearted Polish priest did what he could to shelter the homeless Jews from Hitler's brutality, secretly hiding 2,000 of them in his monastery.

But hiding Jews was risky, to put it mildly. The Nazis were intent on completely ridding the world of the Jewish race; they senselessly slaughtered millions of Jews in their "death camps" scattered across continental Europe. And if they discovered that someone was helping the Jews, the Nazis would turn their wrath on them as well.

Sadly that's exactly what happened in February 1941.

Members of the dreaded Gestapo, Hitler's "secret police," crashed through the gates of Father Kolbe's monastery and arrested the Jews...as well as those who hid them. The merciful and gentle Father Kolbe was rounded up like a criminal and tossed into Pawiak Prison, guilty of only one crime: Helping Jews.

At the prison, he suffered through one interrogation after another. Just when it seemed the nightmare couldn't get worse, it did.

Father Kolbe was transferred to a place of terror and death known as Auschwitz.

Auschwitz was the "crown jewel" in the Nazis' sinister plan to kill every Jew in existence. The huge concentration camp was actually a network of prisons that housed lethal gas chambers where Jews, gypsies, political prisoners, and the physically handicapped were executed. Auschwitz had a notorious reputation; roughly 2.5 million people were brutally murdered within its walls.

Living conditions at Auschwitz were unimaginably cruel. Food supplies were always short, and vicious beatings were always abundant. The combination of the two usually left the prisoners exhausted and susceptible to disease, another rampant killer.

Some of the prisoners, the lucky ones, did manual labor—for instance, gardening and building. Other prisoners were used in horrific "science experiments" that usually ended in their deaths. And some of the prisoners were even forced to work in the gas chambers, herding their friends and family members to their deaths and then cleaning up their remains.

Auschwitz excelled at one thing: Death.

But it was within these deadly walls that Father Kolbe, now known as Prisoner #16670, made his most significant impact.

The middle-aged priest was continually busy at the death camp. He preached the gospel to his fellow prisoners, served the captives Communion, and encouraged them on a daily basis. He heard their confessions and taught them to live like Christ in spite of their awful circumstances. But those were just his priestly duties....

Because he was a prisoner, he also suffered under the torturous workload of his wicked captors. But the anguish inflicted on Father Kolbe was much worse than that of a regular prisoner. The Nazis took great joy in persecuting the priest; they desperately wanted to break him.

Their physical abuse had one aim: to destroy the credibility of the Christian faith he professed. If they could cause him to lash out at them in retaliation, the Nazis could say he was as evil as they were. If they could make him curse God and abandon his faith because of his suffering, they could tell the rest of the prisoners that faith in God meant nothing.

And so the guards assigned Father Kolbe the most grueling manual labor possible, and then released attack dogs on him to make him work even faster. Time and time again, they beat him mercilessly. The Nazis' violence against Kolbe was so great that after one particular beating, his tormentors left him under a bush, assuming he was dead.

The harsh treatment he suffered landed him in one sick ward after another. Most prisoners couldn't survive being sent to the sick wards; disease was everywhere because of the high number of dead bodies and lack of sanitary conditions. Further, because most prisoners ended up dying in the wards, the spiteful guards intentionally decreased the food allotments they received, which made the sick people even weaker.

Why feed someone who can't work? Why feed a lousy prisoner who's just going to be killed anyway?

But even in the infirmary, Father Kolbe led by sacrificial example and deeply impacted those around him. He routinely offered his small portions of food and drink to fellow prisoners and made sure the doctors cared for others before they cared for him. His acts of kindness for complete strangers—many of whom didn't even speak his language—made everyone who met him grateful for the encounter.

At one point, after a particularly vicious beating that landed him in the sick ward, the weak priest was prematurely released from the infirmary and ordered to join a work crew operating outside the prison's walls. Even though Father Kolbe was forced to do backbreaking manual labor with fresh wounds on his tired body, he made gradual improvements in his health.

And then, the improbable happened: One of the prisoners assigned to his work crew seized the opportunity to escape.

At Auschwitz, one escapee meant the death of 10 prisoners.

It was a cruel but extremely effective way to keep prisoners from trying to escape. Sneaking past the armed guards, razor wire, and attack dogs was only part of the struggle. Anyone brave enough to escape also knew they were condemning their friends and loved ones to death.

At the end of that fateful day, the prisoners from Block 14, Father Kolbe's division, were counted once more. One prisoner was still missing.

Such a brazen act got the attention of Commandant Karl Fritsch, the camp deputy, so he personally visited the prison to select those who would die. He arrogantly moved through the ranks of prisoners, pointing to one here and another there, until the grim quota of 10 had been met.

Those not selected for execution breathed a sigh of relief.

Polish army sergeant Francis Gajowniczek had been selected. As the

Nazis dragged him away, he wailed loudly, "My poor wife! My poor children! What will happen to my family?"

The piercing grief of the condemned soldier prompted Father Kolbe to one last act of sacrifice.

The godly priest quietly stepped out of line, took off his cap, and respectfully stood before the commanding officer.

"What do you want, you Polish pig?" demanded Fritsch.

"I am a Catholic priest," said Father Kolbe. "I would like to take his place, because he has a wife and children."

After sizing up the priest, Fritsch eventually waved his hand in compliance, and said, "Away." That one word sealed the fate of Father Maximilian Kolbe.

As Sergeant Gajowniczek was shoved back into the ranks of astounded men who had just witnessed the supreme act of sacrifice, Kolbe and the other nine men were marched to the camp's underground cells. There they would be stripped of all their clothes and subjected to one of the cruelest forms of execution: Starvation.

For days, the men languished in their shared cell. Father Kolbe heard their confessions and prayed with the men, but one by one they succumbed to an excruciating death. Three agonizing weeks later, only Father Kolbe and three others were alive.

But in Auschwitz, death was always near. The cell was needed for a fresh batch of condemned prisoners, so the four men were injected with a lethal dose of carbolic acid. The weakened men died within a matter of minutes.

But Father Kolbe's legacy lives on.

Source: http://itslikethis.org/?p=2974

TRANSITION STATEMENT

Indeed, the greatest sacrifice we can ever make is to lay down our lives for others. This is exactly what Jesus has done for us.

The Bible tells us that Jesus willingly gave his life for ours. Even though he was perfect, he chose to die on the cross for guilty sinners like you and me. Our lives were saved because he gave up his.

APPLICATION AND SCRIPTURE

Romans 5:6-8 reveals the unconditional nature of God's love. The writer, the Apostle Paul, describes the people whom Christ died for. This is his description of humanity—of us:

⁶You see, at just the right time, when we were still powerless, Christ died for the ungodly. ⁷Very rarely will anyone die for a righteous person, though for a good person someone might possibly dare to die. ⁸But God demonstrates his own love for us in this: While we were still sinners, Christ died for us.

I want us to look at three key words to unpack this passage of God's word to us today. The three words—*powerless, sinners,* and the little word *for*—speak volumes.

Powerless

This word in the New Testament is often used to describe the sick and feeble. It's also used in the moral sense to mean the inability to perform your duty or job. Paul is using the term in this passage to say that we have no power to do even one tiny thing to please God or achieve salvation.

For the prisoners in Auschwitz, death was always near and they were powerless to do anything about it. If one prisoner escaped, 10 would die. That was the rule and they couldn't do anything about it. As they stood in line and waited their fate by the guard who would make the call, they were powerless. Even when Polish army sergeant Francis Gajowniczek pleaded for his life, his desperate cry carried no guarantee that the Commandant Karl Fritsch would even listen. He was powerless. But by an act of love, over which Francis had no control, Father Kolbe spoke up and said, "I would like to take his place." That is how Paul sums up our condition in this world. We are powerless. We need someone to save us.

Sinners

We are desperately in need of a change that we can't make, and for the most part we don't want to make. We are neither righteous nor good. And we can try and try to change our conditions, but we are powerless to make a difference.

But something happened. That is when God proved his love for us. Look at verse 7. "Very rarely will anyone die for a righteous person, though for a good person someone might possibly dare to die." How many people would you give your life for? There are those we love, and we would probably be willing to die for them in crises. But in reality, most of us would only be willing to lay down our lives for a handful of others. How many of us would be willing to die for a bunch of people that we don't even know?

God went way beyond what we would do. "But God demonstrates his own love for us in this: While we were still sinners, Christ died for us." (v. 8) He didn't die for his friends. Point of fact, he died for his enemies. The emphasis in this verse is on the fact that we were still sinners when Christ died for us. The beauty is not that Christ should die for us—but that he should do so while we were powerless and rebellious sinners. Why would he do that? Let's look at another word that helps us understand the reason.

For

Paul uses this word several times in Romans 5. This word in the original Greek is so complex that no single English word can completely express what it means. It can be translated, "for the benefit of" or "on behalf of" or "instead of." When the Bible says that Jesus died for you, it means that he died on your behalf, in your place, so that you can enjoy all the benefits of his work.

Let me paraphrase what Paul is saying in Romans 5:8: "But God displayed his own love for us for this reason: While we were still powerless sinners, Christ died instead of us...for our benefit and on our behalf."

CLOSING

How about you? Do you ever become tired of the fact that you keep doing things that you know are wrong? Do you keep feeling that even though you are a pretty good person, there are things in your life that you hate? Do you have feelings, thoughts, actions, and attitudes that you just wish would go away?

Maybe you want to know God, but you feel that he would never want you. The first step in getting to know God is to recognize that you are powerless to forgive your own sin. You must recognize that you are a sinner and that Christ, though he was sinless, paid the ultimate price for your sin—he died for you. You won't know him until you've received the free gift of Jesus Christ. There's no way you can earn God's love because it's not for sale. Nothing we do can make God love us any more than he already does, and there is nothing we can do to make him love us any less. All we can do is put our trust in him.

If you'd like to make that decision right now, pray with me.

Let's pray.

SMALL GROUP QUESTIONS

1. **Around the Circle:** What is the nicest act anyone has ever done for you? How did that make you feel?

2. **Ask Just a Few:** Why do you think Father Kolbe gave his life for Francis?

Jesus did this for us. Romans 5:6-8 reveals the unconditional nature of God's love. The writer, the Apostle Paul, describes the people that Christ died for. This is his description of humanity—of us.

⁶You see, at just the right time, when we were still powerless, Christ died for the ungodly. ⁷Very rarely will anyone die for a righteous person, though for a good person someone might possibly dare to die. ⁸But God demonstrates his own love for us in this: While we were still sinners, Christ died for us.

3. **Ask Just a Few:** According to verse 6, when did Christ die for us? What were we powerless to do?

4. **Ask Just a Few:** According to these verses, whom did Christ die for? Who are sinners? (Look up Romans 3:23 as a cross reference.)

5. **Ask Just a Few:** Since Christ died "instead" of us, what does that do for us?

6. **Around the Circle:** How does it make you feel knowing that Christ gave his life for you, even though you messed up?

7. **Around the Circle:** Forgiveness is free to anyone willing to put his or her trust in Jesus. Would any of you like to receive that forgiveness right now? (Take the pressure off interested parties by suggesting the group members close their eyes and raise their hands if they're interested in receiving Christ.)

10-Minute Talks

24 Messages Your Students Will Love

Jonathan McKee

Sometimes you don't have their attention for very long. Whether you've planned for a short message or your program has run long, a ten-minute talk is sometimes all you have space for in your youth ministry. So make sure you make it ten minutes that really count!

If you need to communicate something meaningful in just a little time, *10-Minute Talks* has just what you need—more than two dozen ready-to-go, story-based talks. With talks for spiritual growth, targeted at your Christian students, and outreach talks, perfect for any teenager, you'll be prepared to give them a bite of truth that they can walk away remembering. Following the method Jesus used most often, these *10-Minute Talks* give you stories that can impact students with one simple point.

Each talk gives you the tools you need to make it count, and the flexibility to make it work for your context. Along with each topic and title, you'll find:

- The Big Idea
- Scripture
- The Story
- The Transition Statement
- Application
- Closing

Don't get caught with nothing to say—or too much to say in the time you've got! Get *10-Minute Talks* and get a meaningful message across quickly!

Available in stores and online!

Getting Students to Show Up

Practical Ideas for Any Outreach Event—from 10 to 10,000

Jonathan McKee

"... Here you can learn how to plan programs that point people to Jesus by hearing others' mistakes and getting useful advice from a savvy veteran."

—YouthWorker Journal

Youth workers often learn how to program outreach events by "trial and error." They need a resource to not only teach them the basics in programming outreach events, but also give them tools and examples that actually work. *Getting Students to Show Up* will help them understand the mindset of this outreach crowd, and give them the tools to plan effective outreach programs.

The book will show them examples of how not to run events, as well as giving them "ready-made" events that work. It will also provide the basics such as the importance of *draw*, and aligning every single element with the events purpose.

Available in stores and online!

Do They Run When They See You Coming?

Reaching Out to Unchurched Teenagers

Jonathan McKee

Five facts about unchurched teenagers:

1. They believe all religions have value.
2. They are spiritual, not religious.
3. They don't know what Christianity really is.
4. They don't know what they believe.
5. They are looking for something that works.

If you want to make an impact on this generation, these are five basic rules you must understand. Author Jonathan McKee writes that by taking the time to learn students' unique situations you show you care about them as people, not as mission projects.

Informative and full of real-life examples, *Do They Run When They See You Coming?* provides vital information you need to better understand students outside your youth group. Yet this book isn't a sociological or marketing survey; the tangible guidelines and methods inside help you get into the mind of unchurched students—so you can get to know their hearts. Because, as every youth worker knows, real ministry is always about getting to the heart.

Connect

Real Relationships in a World of Isolation

Jonathan McKee

In an age where teenagers are deeply engaged in virtual communities and social networks, they're still feeling alone and isolated. It may sound all too simple, but the truth is that you have the opportunity to make a profound impact on the lives of students with the simple act of spending time with them, one-on-one.

Whether you're a volunteer or the lead youth pastor, getting some students to open up and share their lives can be a challenge. In this practical book you'll learn the importance of connecting with students on an individual basis and get helpful ideas on how to engage a variety of students in meaningful dialogue. You'll explore and learn more about connecting with six different types of students, including:

- The "No Way" Kid
- The "Not Interested" Kid
- The "Checking Things Out" Kid
- The "Stagnant" Kid
- The "Growing" Kid
- The "Looking for Ministry" Kid

Connect will walk you through the steps to lead you into relationships with students that go beyond the youth room and impact them into adulthood."

Available in stores and online!

Real Conversations: A DVD Study

Sharing Your Faith Without Being Pushy

Jonathan McKee

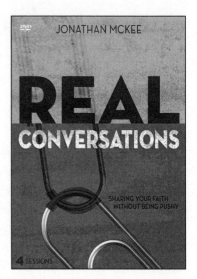

For many teenagers, sharing their faith in Jesus to their friends is an overwhelming and scary prospect. Outreach is inviting their friends to a fun event once a year. In this entertaining DVD training, Jonathan McKee ignites the passion of Christian teenagers to live authentic lives and gives them tools to reach out to their friends in ways that won't give them cold sweats! The message is simple: an authentic faith creates opportunities to talk about Jesus. Students will discover the secret to sharing the reason for the hope that's within them. A participant's guide is also available.

Available in stores and online!

Ministry by Teenagers

Developing Leaders from Within

Jonathan McKee and David R. Smith

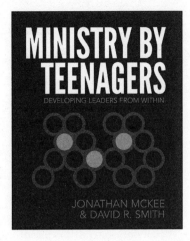

"What would happen if we gave teenagers opportunities to serve and use their gifts in ministry prior to high school graduation? What if we poured into these young leaders, discipling them and doing ministry alongside of them, helping them grow spiritually, seeing and experiencing God working through them? What if we eased back on our ministry to students, supplementing it with ministry by students?"

These compelling questions are at the heart of *Ministry by Teenagers*, and once authors McKee and Smith lay out the "what ifs" they combine their collective experience in youth ministry to provide a practical and detailed guide for "how to." The book is jam-packed with ideas, advice, and resources for:

- Fostering discipleship
- Building student leadership teams
- Identifying student talent
- Helping students discover and use their spiritual gifts
- Creating service teams
- Equipping students to reach their friends

It's a must-have tool for youth workers who want to tap the gold mine of talent, passion, and leadership potential they see every day in young Christians.

Available in stores and online!